Mixing and Mastering with IK Multimedia T-RackS®: The Official Guide

Bobby Owsinski

Course Technology PTR
A part of Cengage Learning

COURSE TECHNOLOGY
CENGAGE Learning

Australia • Brazil • Japan • Korea • Mexico • Singapore • Spain • United Kingdom • United States

COURSE TECHNOLOGY
CENGAGE Learning

Mixing and Mastering with IK Multimedia T-RackS®: The Official Guide
Bobby Owsinski

Publisher and General Manager,
 Course Technology PTR: Stacy L. Hiquet

Associate Director of Marketing: Sarah Panella

Manager of Editorial Services: Heather Talbot

Marketing Manager: Mark Hughes

Executive Editor: Mark Garvey

Project Editor/Copy Editor: Cathleen D. Small

Interior Layout Tech: MPS Limited,
 A Macmillan Company

Cover Designer: Luke Fletcher

Indexer: Larry Sweazy

Proofreader: Laura R. Gabler

T-RackS is a registered trademark of IK Multimedia Production in the United States and other countries. All other trademarks are the property of their respective owners.

All images © Bobby Owsinski unless otherwise noted.

Library of Congress Control Number: 2010928006

ISBN-13: 978-1-4354-5759-1
ISBN-10: 1-4354-5759-5

Course Technology, a part of Cengage Learning
20 Channel Center Street
Boston, MA 02210
USA

Cengage Learning is a leading provider of customized learning solutions with office locations around the globe, including Singapore, the United Kingdom, Australia, Mexico, Brazil, and Japan. Locate your local office at: **international. cengage.com/region**

Cengage Learning products are represented in Canada by Nelson Education, Ltd.

For your lifelong learning solutions, visit **courseptr.com**

Visit our corporate website at **cengage.com**

Printed in the United States of America
2 3 4 5 6 7 12 11

Foreword

As musicians, we live in quite possibly the most exciting era in history. Never before have we had access to such an amazing array of cool gear and access to the professionals who use it every day. What was virtually impossible 10 or even 5 years ago is now an everyday occurrence. Musicians now write, perform, record, mix, master, and distribute their own works, taking full control and ownership of the entire process where desired and reaping tremendous personal reward for their efforts. Thanks to technological advancements and sheer desire and determination, the traditional rulebook has been obliterated, and an entire industry is being transformed, not by a mere few but by the entire population of those who inhabit it. Exciting times indeed.

And what you hold in your hands is no exception.

Ask 18 different mastering professionals what mastering is, and you'll get 18 different answers. The reason is that mastering is both a process and an art form...one that can make a huge difference in how the world receives and perceives your creation. Sure, there is a loose framework of "rules" that roughly define a process, but for the most part, mastering is art. Some refer to it as auditory "magic," a type of voodoo only available to the secret society of the "mastering elite" that reveals the true hidden emotional character of a passage. If that's true, then we'd like to welcome you to the secret society.

This book is the work of one of the most respected recording veterans in the industry, Bobby Owsinski. His recording and mastering credits read like a who's who of the music industry. Once you dig into this material, you'll quickly see why. He's the expert, but he's also accessible, which will make it seem as if you're sitting at the console with him as he helps you navigate through the wonderful world of compressors, EQs, limiters, gates, and meters to create pure tonal magic.

This book was not conceived to be a manual for a particular set of tools (specifically T-RackS 3 Deluxe), but rather as a guide for learning the concepts of mastering and how to apply certain tools to effectively accomplish what you set out to do. Mastering is art, and the better you understand how to apply the tools on your palette, the better your art becomes. You'll learn when to—and when not to—use the tools, what they can and can't do, and then how to creatively apply them to other areas, yielding possibly unexpected pleasing results. You'll quickly realize that once you conquer a particular method or task, there are many ways to approach it.

We sincerely hope you enjoy reading and learning from this book. But most of all, we hope you get real value from it and can incorporate things you learn here into your art, thus helping the industry remain a dynamic, ever-changing, and exciting place to be. We look forward to hearing you.

Sincerely,
The Musicians of IK Multimedia
IK Multimedia. Musicians First.

Acknowledgments

Thanks to Gary Kerzner, Starr Ackerman, and Paul Hudson at IK Multimedia, Mark Garvey and Stacy Hiquet at Course Technology PTR, and Cathleen Small for the great editing job.

About the Author

A longtime music industry veteran, **Bobby Owsinski** started his career as a guitar and keyboard player, songwriter, and arranger, eventually becoming an in-demand producer/engineer working not only with a variety of recording artists, but on commercials, television, and motion pictures as well. One of the first to delve into surround sound music mixing, Bobby has worked on more than a hundred surround projects and DVD productions for a variety of superstar acts.

Using his music and recording experience combined with an easy-to-understand writing style, Bobby has become one of the best-selling authors in the music recording industry. A frequent moderator, panelist, and program director for a variety of industry conferences, Bobby has served as the longtime producer of the annual Surround Music Awards and is one of the executive producers for the *Guitar Universe* and *Desert Island Music* television programs.

Visit Bobby's production blog at bobbyowsinski.blogspot.com, his Music 3.0 blog at music3point0.blogspot.com, and his website at bobbyowsinski.com.

Preface

I must admit that I was pleased when I was approached by IK Multimedia about collaborating on a book about T-RackS 3. I had been using the application for quite some time as a part of my personal software arsenal, so I was already a fan and quite familiar with it.

But I assume that you're just getting into the program if you're reading this book, so let me tell you the reasons why I think T-RackS is such a great app. It's a simple yet powerful stand-alone (that's the key) mastering app that has all of the features you need to do a great mastering job. The metering is extremely sophisticated (just that is worth the price, in my opinion), it's unique in that it has a warm analog sound that's transparent at the same time, and the T-RackS modules also work very well as plug-ins in your favorite DAW during mixing. To be sure, there's a lot of great software that can be used for mastering out there, but none other than T-RackS fits this particular profile.

The reason for the book is that although T-RackS can do wondrous things for your music, it can just as easily take your music in the wrong direction if you're not sure how to drive it. To be sure, T-RackS is extremely powerful, but all of that power won't do you much good if it's misused. Even after writing a best-selling book about mastering (*The Mastering Engineer's Handbook: The Audio Mastering Handbook* [Course Technology PTR, 2007]), I realize that there's an awful lot of misconceptions about what mastering is and what it can do, which is something that this book will try to rectify.

Along the way we'll cover how to use T-RackS during both mixing and mastering and provide some useful tips and tricks for both. And at the end of each chapter, there are a number of questions that will help you to better understand some of the principles of mixing and mastering basics.

While this book does cover some of the basic concepts of mixing and mastering, if you want some greater detail on each subject, take a look at my other books on the subject: *The Mixing Engineer's Handbook* (Course Technology PTR, 2006) and *The Mastering Engineer's Handbook: The Audio Mastering Handbook*. You can read some excerpts from them and my other books at bobbyowsinski.com.

If you also want some daily tips on production and the music business, you can follow my blogs at:

- Bobby Owsinski's Big Picture Blog: bobbyowsinski.blogspot.com
- Bobby Owsinski's Music 3.0 Blog: music3point0.blogspot.com

I'd love to hear your thoughts and suggestions regarding this book, so please feel free to email me at bobby@bobbyowsinski.com.

Bobby Owsinski Bibliography

The Mixing Engineer's Handbook, Second Edition (Course Technology PTR, 2006). The premier book on audio mixing techniques provides all the information you need to take your mixing skills to the next level, along with advice from the world's best mixing engineers.

The Recording Engineer's Handbook, Second Edition (Course Technology PTR, 2009). Revealing the microphone and recording techniques used by some of the most renowned recording engineers, you'll find everything you need to know to lay down great tracks in any recording situation, in any musical genre, and in any studio.

The Mastering Engineer's Handbook: The Audio Mastering Handbook (Course Technology PTR, 2007). Everything you always wanted to know about mastering, from doing it yourself to using a major facility, utilizing insights from the world's top mastering engineers.

The Drum Recording Handbook (with Dennis Moody) (Hal Leonard, 2009). Uncovers the secrets of amazing drum recordings in your recording studio even with the most inexpensive gear. It's all in the technique, and this book and DVD will show you how.

How to Make Your Band Sound Great (Hal Leonard, 2009). This band improvement book and DVD shows your band how to play to its fullest potential. It doesn't matter what kind of music you play, what your skill level is, or if you play covers or your own music, this book will make you tight, it will make you more dynamic, it will improve your show, and it will improve your recordings.

The Studio Musician's Handbook (with Paul Ill) (Hal Leonard, 2009). Everything you wanted to know about the world of the studio musician, including how to become a studio musician, who hires you and how much you get paid, what kinds of skills you need and what gear you must have, the proper session etiquette required to make a session run smoothly, and how to apply these skills in every type of recording session, regardless of whether it's in your home studio or at Abbey Road.

Music 3.0: A Survival Guide to Making Music in the Internet Age (Hal Leonard, 2009). The paradigm has shifted, and everything you knew about the music business has completely changed. Who are the new players in the music business? Why are traditional record labels, television, and radio no longer factors in an artist's success? How do you market and distribute your music in the new music world—and how do you make money? This book answers these questions and more in its comprehensive look at the new music business—Music 3.0.

The Music Producer's Handbook (Hal Leonard, 2010). Reveals the inside information and secrets to becoming a music producer and producing just about any kind of project in any genre of music. Among the topics covered are the producer's responsibilities and all the elements of a typical production, including budgeting, contracts, selecting the studio and engineer, hiring session musicians, and even getting paid! The book also covers the true mechanics of production, from analyzing and fixing the format of a song, to troubleshooting a song when it just doesn't sound right, to getting the best performance and sound out of the band and vocalist.

The Musician's Video Handbook (Hal Leonard, 2010). Describes how the average musician can easily make any of the various types of videos now required by a musical artist either for promotion or for final product. But just shooting a video isn't enough. The book will also demonstrate the tricks and tips used by the pros to make it look professionally done, even with inexpensive gear and not much of a budget.

Contents

Chapter 3
Using T-RackS Dynamics during Mixing   21

Chapter 4
Using the T-RackS EQ and Metering during Mixing   33

Introduction

Introduction: About T-RackS 3

T-RackS 3 is a very powerful stand-alone software mastering application from IK Multimedia, a software developer located in the U.S., Italy, and the United Kingdom.

In addition to the stand-alone app, the modules can also be used as individual VST, AU, or RTAS plug-ins in any of the popular digital audio workstations, such as Pro Tools, Logic, Cubase, SONAR, and most others.

There are two versions of T-RackS 3—the standard version, which comes with four processor modules, and the Deluxe version, which comes with five additional modules. Each of the processing modules is also available individually.

The Technology

One thing that makes all T-RackS versions so popular is the warm analog sound that the processor modules provide, since they closely emulate the circuitry of some of the vintage hardware devices that many pros have come to love. Modeling the sound of a piece of hardware is not a trivial process, but IK Multimedia gets better and better at what amounts to a new art form.

At the heart of this modeling is a technology called Sonic Character Cloning (SCC for short), which is a new analysis method developed by IK that turns the sound of some of your favorite vintage pieces into a mathematical algorithm and provides a software reproduction of the sound right down to the smallest behaviors and nuances.

Here's an overview of the individual modules in T-RackS 3. We'll discuss the stand-alone mode of the app later, in Chapter 7 and in the metering section in Chapter 9.

The Processor Modules

At the heart of T-RackS 3 are nine processor modules that cover compression, limiting, and equalization. Whether these modules are used in the T-RackS stand-alone mode or as individual plug-ins, the operation is the same.

Vintage Tube Compressor 670

The Vintage Tube Compressor 670 is based on what has come to be known as the "Holy Grail" of compressors/limiters—the Fairchild 670. The hardware version of the

670 was originally designed for vinyl disc mastering, but its fast attack and smooth release eventually caused engineers to understand that it had the special ability to add a sort of "glue" to a track that's quite unlike other compressors. With a faithful reproduction of every control (see Figure I.1), the T-RackS Vintage Tube Compressor 670 is an incredibly accurate model that captures all the nuances of one of the best of the few working hardware Fairchild units still available.

Figure I.1   The Vintage Tube Compressor 670.

The 670 Controls

AGC. The AGC (Automatic Gain Control) sets how the channels are compressed.

- Set it to Left/Right for unlinked stereo (independent channel) operation.

- Set it to Link for linked stereo operation (both channels will have identical settings except for Input Gain), and the same amount of gain reduction will always be applied to both channels to ensure stereo image stability.

- Set it to Lat/Vert to have the compressor's two channels work on the Mid and Side portions of the stereo signal. With this mode, you'll be able to separately process your Center (Lat) and Sides (Vert) image of the stereo program.

Left-Lat DC Threshold. This control sets the compression knee, or how suddenly the compressor turns on. A soft knee gradually turns on the compression and makes it less audible as a result.

- Set it fully counterclockwise for maximum softness of the compression knee.

- Set it fully clockwise for maximum hardness of the compression knee.

Right-Vert. This control works the same as Left-Lat DC Threshold for the right channel.

Left-Lat Time Constant. Sets the compressor's release time.

- Positions 1 through 4 use a single time constant, from fast to slow.

■ Positions 5 and 6 use dual time constants and are especially useful for mixed stereo material.

Right-Vert Time Constant. Works the same as Left-Lat Time Constant, only for the right channel.

Left Channel Input Gain. Sets the compressor input gain on the left channel.

■ Set this control to 10 for unity I/O gain when no compression is occurs.

Right Channel Input Gain. Same as the Left Channel Input Gain but for the right channel.

Left-Lat Threshold. Sets the amount of compression.

■ Fully counterclockwise means no compression.

■ Fully clockwise give the maximum possible amount of compression for that signal.

Right-Vert Threshold. Same as Left-Lat Threshold, only for the right channel.

In/Out/Gr Meters.

■ GR (gain reduction, the default mode) indicates the amount of compression in dB. Always use the GR position when setting the amount of compression with the Threshold knobs.

■ When set to In, the VU meters will indicate the amount of incoming audio level.

■ When set to Out, the VU meters will indicate the amount of output audio level.

Output. Sets the output level to within a +/−15 dB range.

Bypass. Completely bypasses the module.

Reset. Sets the compressor back to its default state, which results in about 2 dB of compression at moderate input levels.

■ Clicking on this button again will bring back your settings in case you hit Reset by mistake

Tube Program Equalizer Model EQP-1A

Based on what is universally known as one of the most musical EQs ever made (the Pultec EQP-1A), the EQP-1A processor module is an equalizer that has a sound like no other (see Figure I.2). Extremely accurate modeling of two different hardware units known to have "the sound" results in a processing module with performance that is virtually indistinguishable from the original.

Figure I.2   Tube program equalizer model EQP-1A.

The EQP-1A Controls

Low Frequency. Sets the frequency point for the low shelving Boost and Atten filters at 20, 30, 60, or 100 Hz.

■ Please note that because the Pultec's original circuit was based on an imprecise passive equalization network, the boost and attenuation filters will not exactly cover the same frequency band and therefore will not cancel each other out if set identically, the way most equalizers and filters would.

Low Frequency Boost. Applies a boost with a shelving curve shape to low frequencies selected by the Low Frequency control.

■ Set it to 0 for no boost, 10 for max boost.

Low Frequency Atten. Attenuates the low frequencies selected by the Low Frequency control with a shelving curve shape.

■ Set it to 0 for no attenuation, 10 for max attenuation.

Bandwidth. Widens or narrows the range of frequencies selected by the High Frequency control using a bell curve.

■ The far left position (counterclockwise position) is the widest band or Q, while the far-right position (clockwise position) is the narrowest.

■ This control does not affect the sound of the low-frequency filter or the high-frequency attenuation.

High Frequency. Sets the center frequency of the high-frequency bell boost filter at 3, 4, 5, 8, 10, 12, or 16 kHz.

■ The high-frequency boost and attenuation filter have independent frequency settings.

High Frequency Boost. Applies a high-frequency boost using a bell shape that's centered on the frequency selected by the High Frequency control.

■ Set it to 0 for no boost, 10 for maximum boost.

High Frequency Atten. Attenuates the high frequencies using a shelving curve that begins at the frequency selected by the Atten Sel control.

■ Set it to 0 for no attenuation, 10 for max attenuation.

Atten Sel. Sets the frequency point of the high-frequency attenuation filter at 5, 10, or 20 kHz.

Output. Sets the global equalizer gain from −15 to + 15 dB.

On/Off. Bypasses the unit when set to the Off position.

Reset. Resets the equalizer to its default state with all controls set to flat.

L=R. Indicates the linked-channel mode.

■ Use this setting when you want to apply the exact same equalization to both the left and right channels at the same time.

L/R. Select either the L or R icon when you want to tweak the equalization independently on the left or right channel.

M/S. Inserts a Mid-Side matrix into the processing chain that allows you to equalize the center or the sides of the stereo program.

■ Select the M to equalize the center (Mid) of your stereo image or the S to equalize the sides.

■ The L and R icons will be replaced by M and S when in this mode.

Opto Compressor

Optical compression has a special sonic character that many engineers love. This analog-modeled module (see Figure I.3) faithfully re-creates the particular sound that characterizes the best opto compressors.

The Opto Compressor Controls

Input. Sets the input level of the compressor from −24 to +24 dB.

Ratio. Sets the gain reduction ratio of the compressor.

■ Use low values when gentle and transparent compression is required and higher values for more powerful and obvious compression.

■ Ratio range is from 1:1 (no compression) to 30:1 (limiting).

Figure I.3   Opto Compressor.

Attack. Sets the attack time of the compressor from 0 to 50 ms.

■ Be aware that extremely fast attack values (less than 5 ms) may result in certain sounds having a slight bit of distortion.

Release. Sets the compressor release time from 30 ms to 5 seconds.

Compression. Sets the amount of compression that's applied to the signal.

■ Fully counterclockwise means no compression, fully clockwise means full compression.

In/Out/Gr Meters. Provides an indication of the amount of input, output, and gain reduction.

■ GR (gain reduction, the default position) indicates the amount of compression in dB. Always use the GR position when setting the desired compression amount with the Compression knob.

■ When set to In, the VU meters will indicate the input audio level.

■ When set to Out, the VU meters will indicate the level at the output of the compressor.

Output. Sets the compressor output level from +24 to −24 dB.

Bypass. Bypasses the Opto Compressor module when selected.

Reset. Sets the compressor back to its default state, which results in about 2 dB of compression at moderate input levels.

■ Clicking on this button again will bring back your settings in case you hit Reset by mistake

L=R. Indicates the linked-channel mode.

■ The compression will be the same on both channels, which will avoid stereo image shifts.

L/R. Select either the L or the R icon when you want to tweak the compression on the left or right channel independently.

M/S. Inserts a Mid-Side matrix into the processing chain that allows you to compress the center or the sides of the stereo program.

- Select the M to compress the center (Mid) of your stereo image or the S to compress the sides.

- The L and R icons will be replaced by M and S when in this mode.

Brickwall Limiter

The Brickwall Limiter (see Figure I.4) is a "look-ahead"-type limiter that prevents the signal from exceeding a maximum signal level (the "brick wall"). Although hardware brickwall limiters exist, this is one area where software has always outperformed hardware. Selectable algorithms that allow you to match the best limiting style for each program type are a unique feature of this T-RackS module.

- IMPORTANT: This processor should be always used at the end of your T-RackS mastering chain because it has special features to keep the final output level from exceeding 0 dB FS and overloading.

- The D/A Distortion Protection option that can be enabled from the Preferences panel (see Chapter 7) does *not* have the proper effect when this module is not used at the end of the processing chain.

Figure I.4   The Brickwall Limiter.

The Brickwall Limiter Controls

Gain Reduction. Indicates the amount of limiting that is currently occurring in the gain reduction element of the limiter.

- Limiting obtained when using the Saturation or Clipping styles is *not* shown by this meter.

Input. Sets the input level for the limiter and the volume increase that the limiter will provide as a result.

Attack Time. Sets the limiter attack time.

- Depending on how much limiting you apply, it may be necessary to increase the attack time in order to preserve the sense of impact with transient material, such as drums.

Release Time. Sets the limiter release time.

- The longer the release time, the softer the limiter will sound.

- Short release times will make the limiter more suitable for rock, R&B, pop, and so on, because it will sound punchier.

- Longer release times will make the limiter more suitable for music that is generally more quiet, such as jazz, classical, acoustic, and so on, because it's smoother sounding.

Style. Sets the algorithm style of the limiter. Options are:

- **Clean.** The cleanest and most transparent style, Clean is useful for genres where the absence of distortion is a must.

- **Advanced 1, 2, 3, 4.** These styles use a mix between warm and smooth saturation and digital limiting. All offer more punch and color than the Clean style.

- **Sat 1, 2, 3.** These styles use various forms of saturation for limiting. The Gain Reduction meter will not indicate any reduction because the gain reduction element isn't inserted when using these styles.

- **Clipping.** Features straight digital 0 dB FS clipping. Once again, no gain reduction shown.

Output Ceiling. Sets the absolute maximum audio level, which will never be exceeded.

- Typically set to −0.1 or 0.2 dB.

- If D/A Distortion Protection is selected in the Preferences, this can be left at 0 dB.

Output. Indicates the limiter output audio level.

Bypass. Bypasses the Brickwall Limiter module when selected.

Reset. Sets the limiter back to its default state.

- Clicking on this button again will bring back your settings in case you hit Reset by mistake.

L=R. Select the L or R icons to tweak the limiter's left or right channels independently.

Linear Phase Equalizer

The Linear Phase Equalizer is an accurate, high-definition, high-precision EQ (see Figure I.5) that has six identical frequency bands featuring a wide range of filter types. Each band covers the entire frequency spectrum, and frequency overlap of other bands is possible. What makes this EQ unique is that it's switchable between minimum and linear phase characteristics for unusually clean and transparent operation.

Figure I.5   Linear Phase Equalizer.

The Linear Phase Equalizer Controls

Gain/Res 1 through 6. Sets the gain from −15 to +15 dB when the band is set to Peaking or Shelving.

■ When the band is set to high- or low-pass filters, this knob will control the resonance (a particular frequency that's accentuated).

Freq 1 through 6. Sets the center or cutoff frequency for the band.

■ All bands can span from 10 Hz to 20 kHz.

Q 1 through 6. Sets the bandwidth of the Peaking filters.

■ The Q (bandwidth) ranges from 0.2 (very wide) to 20 (very narrow).

■ When bands are set to Shelving, this knob will set the shape of the shelving filter from gentle to steep and resonant, spanning from 0.2 to 3.

Band On/Off. Each band can be turned On or Off independently.

■ All bands are Off at startup.

■ The button turns green when the band is On.

Band Filter Type. Each band can be set to work as:

■ A peaking filter (default for bands from 2 to 5)

■ A shelving filter (defaults for bands 1 and 6)

■ A high- or low-pass filter (see Figure I.6)

Figure I.6 The high-pass filter.

Output. Sets the equalizer output level from −15 to +15 dB.

Output Meter. A peak level meter that indicates the equalizer output level.

Linear Phase. Sets the phase characteristic of the equalizer.

- When Off is selected, the equalizer performs with minimum phase characteristics.

- When On is selected, the equalizer has completely linear phase.

- IMPORTANT: Linear Phase can be activated only if the Oversampling + Linear Phase option in the Preferences is checked (see Chapter 7).

Curve Display. Shows the resulting equalization curve for both channels.

- Individual EQ points can be dragged to set both the Gain and Frequency without using the equalizer knobs.

Bypass. Completely bypasses the equalizer.

On/Off. Bypasses the unit when set to the Bypass position.

Reset. Resets the equalizer to its default state with all controls set to flat.

L=R. Indicates the linked-channel mode.

- Use this setting when you want to apply the exact same equalization to both the left and right channels at the same time.

L/R. Select either the L or R icon when you want to tweak the equalization independently on the left or right channel.

M/S. Inserts a Mid-Side matrix into the processing chain that allows you to equalize the center or the sides of the stereo program.

- Select the M to equalize the center (Mid) of your stereo image or the S to equalize the sides.

- The L and R icons will be replaced by M and S when in this mode.

Classic Compressor

The T-RackS Classic Tube Compressor (see Figure I.7) emulates some of the classic, analog, high-end vintage gear that provides that big, warm sound typical of highly acclaimed hardware devices. This compressor has some unique features not usually found on typical compressors, such as the sidechain high-pass filter and the Stereo Enhancement control, that give it additional flexibility beyond what most compressors provide.

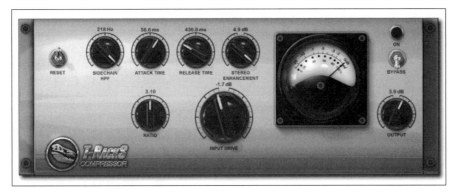

Figure I.7   Classic Compressor.

The Classic Compressor Controls

Sidechain HPF. Adds a high-pass filter to the detector stage of the compressor. The detector stage is where the compressor analyzes the incoming signal and determines how much gain reduction to apply.

- When the frequency is increased, the variable high-pass filter prevents the pumping and breathing effect that's mainly caused by the source material's low-end content.

- The higher the setting, the softer and more inaudible the compression will be.

- At very low settings, the compression will be much more aggressive and noticeable.

- Use lower settings when you want to hear the compression effect and use higher values for a more gentle sound.

Attack Time. Adjusts the attack time of the compressor.

- With higher values, transients will pass unaltered through the compressor.

- With lower values, the gain reduction will respond more quickly, and transients will be more affected. Value range is from 15 ms to 80 ms.

- While adjusting, check above the knob to see the attack time value you're setting.

Ratio. Sets the gain reduction ratio of the compressor.

- Lower values provide a gentler and less noticeable compression effect.

- Higher values provide a more aggressive compression effect.

- The gain reduction ratio is limited to a maximum value of 5:1.

- If you're not sure which ratio control value to use, begin with this control set at 2 or 3.

Release Time. Adjusts the release time of the compressor.

- The recovery time will be longer, and the compression will be less noticeable with longer release times.

- The recovery time will be shorter, and the average loudness will be higher with shorter release times.

- The range is from 70 ms to 1.5 seconds.

Input Drive. Controls the amount of signal that drives the compressor's input.

- There is no traditional "threshold" control, so the amount of compression is determined by the strength of input signal.

- Range is from −18 dB to +18 dB.

Stereo Enhancement. Affects the stereo imaging of the mix.

- Increasing the value will increase the stereo width and vice versa.

- Value range is from −5 to +5 dB, where 0 dB has no effect.

Gain Reduction Meter. Indicates the amount of gain reduction in dB.

- There is no compression when the meter shows 0 dB.

- Indicates the amount of compression in dB.

Output. Sets the compressor output level.

Bypass. Bypasses the compressor module when selected.

Reset. Sets the compressor back to its default state, which results in about 2 dB of compression at moderate input levels.

- Clicking on this button again will bring back your settings in case you hit Reset by mistake

Classic Multiband Limiter

This three-band peak limiter (see Figure I.8) can make a mix louder than other single-band limiters by reducing unwanted peaks in individual frequency bands rather than over the entire mix. With the Multiband Limiter, leaving the Output knob set to 0 dB prevents the limiter's output signal from going beyond −0.05 dB FS.

Figure I.8 Classic Multiband Limiter.

The Multiband Limiter Controls

Single Band Level. These three knobs set the level of the three bands, which is very useful to obtain the correct level of each band after limiting.

■ This can be used as a very broad tone control tool on the mix.

Single Band Threshold. These three knobs set the limiting amount for each individual band.

■ Lowering the threshold will cause the limiting of that band to increase.

Cross-Over Points. These two controls set the two frequency split points between the bands.

■ Use the Cross-Over controls to define a particular band.

Release Time. This is the amount of time the limiter will take to return to normal gain after peak limiting has occurred.

■ Check the numeric display to see the release time value.

■ Value range is from 60 ms to 1.6 seconds.

Input Drive. Controls the amount of signal that drives the Multiband Limiter input.

■ Sets the exact threshold point where limiting begins.

■ The higher the Input Drive is set, the more the peaks will be limited, and the louder the output will be.

■ Value range is from −10 dB to + 15 dB.

■ Values appear above the Drive knob.

Overload. Affects the way the Multiband Limiter reduces peaks.

■ Lower values result in more frequent gain reduction by the limiter.

■ Higher values result in less frequent gain reduction but more frequent clipping.

■ Setting to a higher value results in a louder signal but more clipping across the 0-dB level.

Gain Reduction Meter. Shows the amount of gain reduction in dB.

■ When limiting does not occur, the meter shows 0 dB.

■ When limiting occurs, the meter indicates the amount of limiting in dB.

■ Shows the average value of limiting of all three frequency bands.

Output. Sets the compressor output level.

Bypass. Bypasses the compressor module when selected.

■ When the LED is lit, the Limiter is On.

■ To bypass the limiter module, click the switch so that the LED is Off.

Reset. Sets the compressor back to its default state, which results in about 2 dB of compression at moderate input levels.

■ Clicking on this button again will bring back your settings in case you hit Reset by mistake.

Classic Clipper

This module (see Figure I.9) is useful when you need to eliminate the peaks that keep the average level of a signal too low. Peak clipping is very often used in mastering because in most cases it's more transparent than peak limiting.

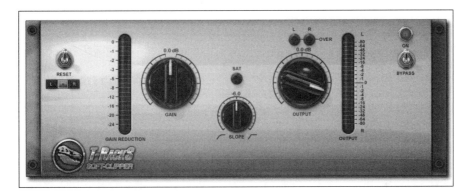

Figure I.9 Classic Clipper.

The Classic Clipper Controls

Gain. Adjusts the level of the signal injected into the clipper stage of the module.

■ Determines the quantity of saturation applied to the audio.

Gain Reduction Meter. Indicates the amount of gain reduction.

Slope. Adjusts the clipping stage's shape from a straight digital hard clip (fully clockwise) to an ultra-soft non-clipping mode (fully counterclockwise).

■ Depending on music styles, the clipping can be less noticeable either with softer or harder shapes, which is why this control is continuously adjustable.

■ Only your ears can detect the optimal clipping shape for the piece of music on which you're working.

■ Use a middle value such as 3 dB as a starting point.

Sat. Indicates that the signal is in the non-linear saturation zone.

Output. Internally calibrated so that the output of the clipper will never overload.

■ Regardless of the input level and the position of the Gain knob, the level will never exceed 0 dB from this module due to the internal 0.05 dB FS ceiling, but only if the Output knob is set at 0 dB.

Output Meter. Indicates the stereo peak output level, with the left channel on the top and the right channel on the bottom.

Over. These two LEDs, separate for left and right channels, light up *only* when a digital overload at the clipper outputs has occurred.

■ In theory, they should never light.

■ Adjust the Output control to ensure that they stay off with as high a level as possible.

Bypass. Bypasses the Clipper module when selected.

Reset. Sets the compressor back to its default state, which results in about 2 dB of compression at moderate mix levels.

■ Clicking on this button again will bring back your settings in case you hit Reset by mistake.

Classic Equalizer

The T-RackS Classic Equalizer (see Figure I.10) consists of a multiband EQ featuring high- and low-pass filters, two shelving filters, and two overlapping parametric equalizers. The filters include:

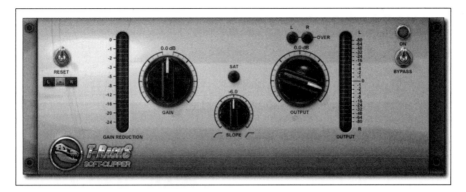

Figure I.10   Classic Equalizer.

- Fourth-order high-pass filter with a variable frequency knee from 16 Hz to 5.3 kHz.

- Low-shelving type filter with a variable frequency knee from 30 Hz to 200 Hz.

- Low-mid peaking type filter with a variable frequency knee from 33 Hz to 5.4 kHz, variable Q.

- High-mid peaking type filter with a variable frequency knee from 200 Hz to 17.5 kHz, variable Q.

- High-shelving type filter with a variable frequency knee from 750 Hz to 8.5 kHz.

- Fourth-order low-pass filter with a variable frequency knee from 200 Hz to 18 kHz.

The Classic EQ Controls

Low Cut Band On/Off. Turns the filter on or off.

- When the filter is active, the button is highlighted in yellow.

Low Cut. Adjusts this frequency of the high-pass filter.

- Sweep range is from 16 Hz to 5.3 kHz.

Low Band On/Off. Turns the filter on or off.

- When the filter is active, the button is highlighted in yellow.

Low Freq. Adjusts the frequency range of the low-shelving filter.

- All frequencies up to this value will be boosted or reduced.

- The cutoff frequency can be set anywhere from 30 Hz to 200 Hz.

Low Gain. Boosts or cuts the level of the band.

- The range is −15 dB to +15 dB.

Low Mid Band On/Off. Turns the filter on or off.

■   When the filter is active, the button is highlighted in yellow.

Low Mid Freq. Adjusts the center frequency of the Low-Mid peaking filter.

■   Range is 33 Hz to 5.4 kHz.

Low Mid Gain. Boosts or cuts the level of the band.

■   The range is −15 dB to +15 dB.

Low Mid Q. Sets the bandwidth of the peaking filter from 0.2 (broad) to 20 (sharp).
Hi Mid Band On/Off. Turns the filter on or off.

■   When the filter is active, the button is highlighted in yellow.

Hi Mid Freq. Adjusts the center frequency of the Hi-Mid peaking filter.

■   Range is from 750 Hz to 17.5 kHz.

Hi Mid Gain. Boosts or cuts the level of the band.

■   The range is −15 dB to +15 dB.

Hi Mid Q. Sets the bandwidth of the peaking filter from 0.2 (broad) to 20 (sharp).
Hi Band On/Off. Turns the filter on or off.

■   When the filter is active, the button is highlighted in yellow.

Hi Freq. Adjusts the frequency range of the high-shelving filter.

■   Range is from 200 to 18 kHz.

Hi Gain. Boosts or cuts the level of the band.

■   The range is −15 dB to +15 dB.

Hi Cut Band On/Off. Turns the filter on or off.

■   When the filter is active, the button is highlighted in yellow.

Hi Cut. Adjusts the cut-off frequency of the low-pass filter.

■   Range is from 200 to 18 kHz.

Output. Sets the equalizer output level from −5 to +15 dB.

Curve Display. Shows the resulting equalization curve for both channels.

■ Individual EQ points can be dragged to set both the gain and frequency without using the equalizer knobs.

Bypass. Completely bypasses the equalizer.

On/Off. Bypasses the unit when set to the Bypass position.

Reset. Resets the equalizer to its default state with all controls set to flat.

L=R. Indicates the linked-channel mode.

■ Use this setting when you want to apply the exact same equalization to both the left and right channels at the same time.

L/R. Select either the L or the R icon when you want to tweak the equalization independently on the left or right channel.

M/S. Inserts a Mid-Side matrix into the processing chain that allows you to equalize the center or the sides of the stereo program.

■ Select the M to equalize the center (Mid) of your stereo image or the S to equalize the sides.

■ The L and R icons will be replaced by M and S when in this mode.

Latency

Latency is the processing time of an application or module. It's usually not much of a problem when mastering, especially in the stand-alone mode of T-RackS, but it may become an issue when the processor modules are used as plug-ins. To cover all latency possibilities, T-RackS 3 has three different latencies available, depending on which of the following preferences is selected:

■ **Lowest Latency.** In this mode, the total T-RackS 3 latency is 132 samples, which is extremely low. Use this setting when you need T-RackS 3 to have the shortest possible latency (such as when you want to use a processor in a real-time monitor mix during recording).

■ **Oversampling.** This delivers higher-quality audio processing to all T-RackS 3 modules but increases latency to 1,284 samples.

■ **Oversampling + Linear Phase.** Use this setting when the maximum audio quality is needed and latency is not a problem (such as during mastering). *The Linear Phase button on T-RackS 3 Linear Phase Equalizer will only work when this setting is selected.* In this mode, the T-RackS total latency is 19,684 samples, or nearly a half-second at a sample rate of 44.1 kHz.

Remember that not all digital audio workstations can compensate for a latency as high as nearly 20,0000 samples (almost half a second at a 44.1-kHz sample rate). This won't be a problem during mastering, but you might want to reduce the T-RackS 3 total latency in the Preferences panel if you need to process tracks that must remain time-aligned to other ones (such as when using T-RackS in mixing). Normally this won't be a problem, since most DAWs can compensate for latency levels of 128 or 2,304 samples (lowest latency/oversampling).

The highest latency level (about 20,000 samples) is only needed when you must use the Linear Phase equalizer, and this is typically only used in mastering, where the latency normally doesn't need to be compensated for.

Plug-In Use

The T-RackS processor modules can be used in two ways—as individual plug-ins or in a mini version of the stand-alone module used for mastering (see Figure I.11). If the stand-alone module is used as a plug-in, it's possible to use multiple processors in the signal chain. Use this mode with care because of the increased demands on your computer processor and a possible increase in latency on that particular channel.

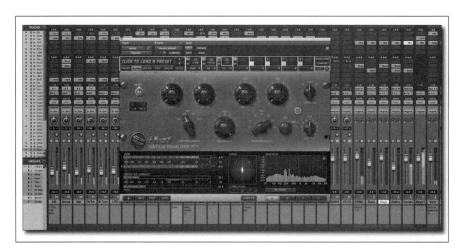

Figure I.11   The stand-alone module used as a plug-in.

1 Mix Preparation

A trait of A-list mixers is their preparation of the source material before the mix begins. Sure, some things will change as the mix goes along, but almost all mix veterans have a starting place that they're comfortable with. This not only saves time later, but it helps keep them sane in the process.

We can break mix preparation down into three categories: technical prep, setup prep, and physical prep. Let's take at look at each.

Technical Prep

Technical preparation is the most mundane of all the tasks. So mundane, in fact, that many A-listers either hire someone or have their assistant do all of this work. That being said, the technical prep may be the most important time you spend on some projects, because it's where you tighten up the individual performances and take them to a new level.

Make a Copy of the Session

The first thing is to make a copy of your session and label it in such a fashion that you can tell what it's for. Something like "songname edits 4-4-11" or "songname voc comp" tells you exactly what's happening at a glance. I like to put the date in the name as well. If I have multiple versions of the session in one day, I'll differentiate one from another with letters of the alphabet at the end, such as "songname edits 4-4-11a," "songname edits 4-4-11b," and so on.

While you're at it, make a copy of the session file on another hard drive, flash drive, online backup, or any place that you can easily grab it if for some reason you find the file you're working on is suddenly corrupted.

Tweak the Timing

No matter how great the players on the session are, there's always some portion of a player's recording that doesn't feel quite right. The exception is that you have enough time to have the musician play his or her part until it's perfect, or you punch in all the suspect parts as you go along.

Usually, the timing of the basic tracks will be tweaked right after your tracking session so you have a solid rhythm section to overdub against, but if you've not done that, or

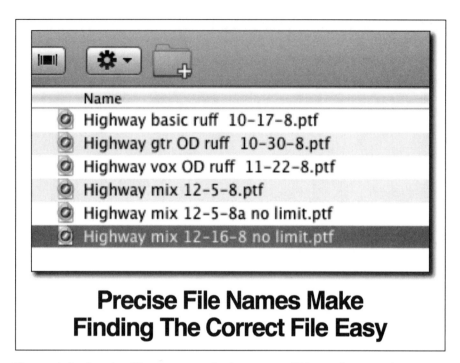

Figure 1.1   Precise file names make it easy to differentiate versions.

you're just now discovering some sections that don't feel right (which happens a lot), prepare for the joys of slipping and sliding time.

Here's a list of some of the dos and don'ts for tweaking timing.

- **Don't edit by eye.** You can't edit successfully by just trying to line everything up to the kick and snare. Often, tracks that look perfectly lined up don't sound or feel right. That's why listening is more important than looking. Turn your head away from the monitor and just listen before and after you move anything.

- **Every beat doesn't have to be perfect.** In fact, if it's too perfect, you'll suck the life out of the performance. Unless something really jumps out as being out of time, you might get away with leaving it as is. Another way is to just line up downbeats and any major accents. That gives you the best of both worlds—a loose feel that still sounds tight.

- **Copy and paste another section.** If you have to make too many edits to a particular section, chances are it won't sound as good when you're finished as just finding a similar section in another part of the song and pasting it in over the area that's suspect. It's a lot faster and easier to do, and it will probably sound cleaner and groove better as well.

- **Be careful with the bass.** Many times the bass will speak better if it's a few milliseconds behind the kick drum rather than right with it. It still sounds tight, but both the kick and the bass will be more distinct.

- **Listen against the drums.** If you listen to the track that you're editing all by itself, you can be fooled into thinking that the timing is corrected, especially if you're editing to a grid. The real proof, though, is when you listen against the drums. If the instrument sounds great by itself and great with the drums, you're home free.

- **Trim the releases.** This is one of the best things you can do to tighten up a track. Everyone is hip to tightening up the attacks, but it's the releases that really make the difference. Regardless of whether it's an accent played by the full band, the song ending, or a vocal or guitar phrase, make sure that the releases are pretty much the same length. If one is longer than the rest, trim it back and fade it so it sounds natural. If one is a lot shorter than the rest, use a time-correction plug-in to lengthen it a bit (see Figure 1.2).

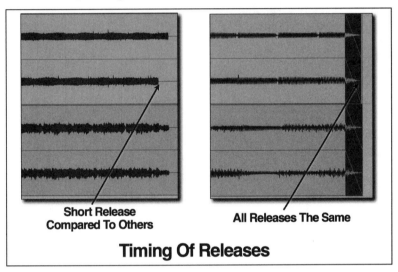

Figure 1.2   Timing of releases.

Of course, if you're using loops or MIDI instruments, you've probably quantized things to the track by now. If you haven't, now's the time.

Eliminate Noises

Now is the time to clean up each individual track. While the noises might not sound too bad with the rest of the track, after everything is mixed and mastered, you might be surprised by how something that was buried can come to the forefront. Also, by eliminating any extraneous noises, all the tracks magically sound distinct and uncluttered.

- **Trim the heads and tails.** Trim all the extra record time at the beginning and end of each track, regardless of whether it was recorded during basics or overdubs. Add a fade-in and fade-out to eliminate any edit noise.

- **Cross-fade your edits.** One of the biggest problems for A-list mixers is when they get a session that's full of edits to make the track sound tight, but the edits click and pop because they don't contain any cross-fades. Even if you can't hear a click or pop, it's a good practice to have a short cross-fade on every edit to eliminate the possibility of an unwanted noise (see Figure 1.3).

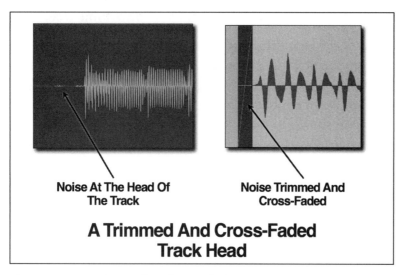

Noise At The Head Of
The Track

Noise Trimmed And
Cross-Faded

**A Trimmed And Cross-Faded
Track Head**

Figure 1.3   A trimmed and cross-faded track head.

■ **Delete extra notes from MIDI tracks.** Delete any extra "split" notes that were mistakenly played. You might not hear them when all the instruments are playing, but just like the noise at the beginning of tracks, they have a tendency to come to the forefront after things get compressed.

Comping

Comping shouldn't be left for mixing, as it's something that's normally taken care of directly after an overdub session for the vocal, guitar or anything else that required multiple takes. That being said, if you still have some vocal or overdub comping to do, now's the time.

Tuning

Inevitably, there's always a note that's a bit sour and needs tuning. Whether you use Auto-Tune, Elastic Audio, or any other pitch correction plug-in, make sure that the timing isn't thrown off when the note is shortened or lengthened.

Setup Prep

This is the "housecleaning" stage where you get everything in the session nice and tidy before you commit to the actual process of mixing. The idea is to make everything easy to locate during the mix.

Make a Copy

As before, it's best to make a copy of the session that's designated as the "mix" ("songtitle mix") so it's easy to see and locate at a later time. This also keeps your previous session safe if you ever have to go back to it.

Delete Empty Tracks

Empty, unused tracks take up space in your edit and mix windows and aren't doing anything useful. It's okay to have empty tracks that you're saving for an instrument when you track or overdub, but if you've gotten this far without using them, you don't need them now. Eliminate them.

Deactivate and Hide Unused Tracks

If there are tracks that are copies or ones that you know you won't be using, deactivate them and hide them so they don't get in the way. Just hiding them isn't enough—they'll still soak up system resources that might be needed later, especially if you use a lot of plug-ins. Make sure you deactivate them.

Arrange the Track Order

Although the track order isn't critical, it will help you move the mix along faster if like instruments are grouped together. This means all the guitars are next to each other, drums and percussion are next to one another, and the vocals are together.

Color-Code the Tracks

If your DAW allows it, color-coding your tracks also makes things a bit easier to find. This means that all the drums would be one color, guitars another, the vocals another, and so on.

Insert Section Markers

Section markers are one of the big timesavers in any DAW. Insert a marker just before each new section (usually a bar or two before works well), as well as any other points in the song that you might want to quickly find during mixing, such as drum fills, accents, or even the halfway point in a section.

Label the Tracks

Many workstations automatically assign a name to new tracks that have just been recorded, but they hardly ever relate to the track. So you don't mistake one track for another and adjust the parameters of the wrong track during the mix, clearly label all the tracks. If the track's name currently is something like "gt012," label it something easy to read, such as "guitar" or "gtr." You'll be happy you did later.

Set Up Groups

Groups are often overlooked, but they're extremely useful during mixing for a number of reasons (see Figure 1.4). First of all, groups allow you to separate elements of the mix in order to make the mix easier to adjust later. Secondly, many times it's a lot easier and better sounding to compress or put an effect on an entire group rather than on each individual instrument (although sometimes both works pretty well).

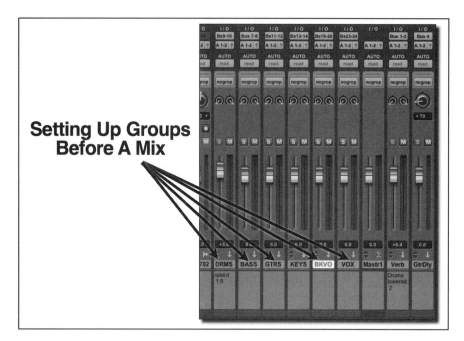

Figure 1.4 Groups set up before a mix.

Typical groups would pertain to any element that has more than one instrument or track, such as Drums, Guitars (if there's more than one or they're in stereo), Lead Vocals (if there's a double), Background Vocals, Horns, Strings, and Synths.

By setting up the groups ahead of time and assigning the particular channels to them, your mix will be both faster and smoother.

Set Up Effects

Most mixers have a standard effects starting point for mixing. One that I've seen that works well even for tracking and overdubs is:

- **For drums.** A reverb using a dark room set to about 1.5 seconds of decay with a pre-delay of 20 milliseconds.

- **For all other instruments.** A plate with about 1.8 seconds of decay and a pre-delay of 20 milliseconds.

- **For vocals.** A delay of about 220 milliseconds.

It's amazing how well these settings work without any tweaking, but to make everything fit better, you can time the delay and pre-delays to the song, but keep the parameters close to the settings above. For instance, if the only delay in the 220-ms region is a 232-ms quarter-note triplet, that's the one to use. The decay is set so that a snare drum hit just about fades out by the time the next one comes around.

Another common setup is two reverbs and two delays, set like:

- **Short Reverb** - a room program with the decay set from 0.5 to 1.5 seconds of decay with a short pre-delay timed to the track.

- **Long Reverb** - a plate or hall program with a decay set from 1.5 to 4 seconds of decay and a pre-delay of as little as 0 or as much as 150 ms timed to the track. (This depends on your taste and what's right for the song.)

- **Short Delay** - a delay of about 50 to 200 milliseconds.

- **Long Delay** - a delay from about 200 to 400 milliseconds.

Of course, this is only a starting point. You might find your own particular starting point uses a lot more effects, or you may prefer to add effects as the need arises during the mix. Regardless, if you have at least some effects set up before you start the mix, you won't have to break your concentration to set them up later.

Assign the Channels   There are some tracks that you know ahead of time will be assigned to a certain effect (such as the drums or snare to a short reverb), so you might as well set that up now as well. Don't forget the panning.

Set Up Compressors and Limiters

Once again, there are some channels that you pretty much know ahead of time will need a compressor inserted, such as the kick, snare, bass, and vocal. It's best to insert it into the signal chain of the channel now, but leave it bypassed until you decide you need it.

If you're a proponent of mixing from the beginning with a stereo buss limiter, now's the time to insert that as well. We'll cover stereo buss compression by itself in Chapter 5, "Mix Buss Compression."

Physical Prep

Now that your DAW session is set up, it's best to take a break and get yourself physically and mentally prepared. Regardless of how much time you spend on a mix, it's mentally taxing because of the focus and concentration that it commands.

Get Comfortable

You're going to be here for a while, so it's best to be comfortable. Change into some comfy clothes, get the temperature of the room just right, and adjust the lighting so it's easy to see the various monitor screen(s). Get some coffee, tea, or soft drinks ready, as well as something to snack on later.

Note Taking

Make sure that you have a pen and a pad of paper to take notes during the session. Post-it notes can also be helpful. If you have a hardware controller, a roll of console tape

(Permacel 724—tape that can be reapplied without leaving any sticky residue behind) will be essential to mark it as needed.

Turn Off the Internet

The greatest time-suck for just about any kind of work is the Internet. It's just too easy to check your email or Facebook or go down the rabbit-hole of surfing the Web when you take a break. It's one of the most difficult things to stay away from these days, but you'll get a lot more work done if you can avoid firing it up in the first place.

Play Something You Know

This may be the single most important piece of advice during mix prep. Play a song or a mix (or both) that you know well before you begin to mix to give you a reference point. This will calibrate your ears to your monitors and keep you from over- or under-EQing as you go along.

As you can see, it's a lot of work setting up for a mix sometimes, but if you can persevere and get it all out of the way, you'll find that your mix will go faster and smoother, and your end product will be a lot closer to what you want it to be.

Summary Questions

You can find answers to the Summary Questions in the Appendix at the end of this book.

1.   What are the three categories of mix preparation?

2.   Why is it important to make a copy of your session and rename it while prepping?

3.   Why is editing the timing of a track by eye dangerous?

4.   List four concerns when tweaking the timing of a track.

5.   How do you tighten up the releases of a track?

6.   What's the reason for eliminating the various noises of a track?

7.   List five preparation items for setup.

8.   If you're not using a track, why should it be deactivated and hidden?

9.   Why are section markers so useful?

10. Why are mix groups so useful?

2 Monitoring

It's surprising how little thought is put into our monitors and listening environment sometimes, considering that a mixer depends upon his monitoring conditions more than just about anything else that goes into mixing. If the monitors don't work with the environment, or if the mixer doesn't interact well with the monitors, then any other tips and techniques that you might learn won't count for much. That's why this chapter is dedicated to some basic monitoring setup and listening techniques. Don't let their simplicity fool you; these easy steps can make a big difference in exactly what you're hearing.

Choosing Your Monitors

So which speaker is best for you to monitor on? Certainly there are plenty of choices, and there is clearly no single favorite among the great mixers. Probably as close to a standard that we've ever had is the Yamaha NS-10M, closely followed by the Auratone (see Figure 2.1) during their peak in the '70s. Since both speakers are no longer made, they're becoming less and less of a standard with each passing month.

Tips for Choosing a Set of Monitors

It's surprising that so many monitors are chosen based on the words of a review or word of mouth, since they're such a personal item. Here are some things to think about before you purchase a monitor.

1. **Don't choose a monitor because someone else is using it.** Monitors are a lot like guitars. Just because Jimmy Page uses a Les Paul doesn't mean that it's right for you. It might be too heavy for your frame, the neck might be too wide, and the sound might not be a good match for the type of music you're playing. It's the same with a monitor. Just because your favorite mixer uses a set of Genelec 1032As, it doesn't mean that they'll be right for you, too. You may hear differently, your hearing experience is different, the match with your room might not work, the match with the type of music you work on might not be ideal, and if they're unpowered, you may not have the same amp to drive them with, so they'll sound different as a result.

Figure 2.1   An Auratone Sound Cube.

2. **Listen to the monitors before you buy them.** Before the pros purchase a monitor, they take their time and listen to them under a wide range of conditions, so why shouldn't you? Okay, you might not have the luxury of living near a big media center with lots of pro audio dealers, and even if you do, you may not have a relationship with one that allows you a personal demo in your own environment. But that shouldn't stop you from listening. This is a serious purchase, so don't take it lightly. Take a trip to your local pro audio or music store and prepare to spend some time listening. Listen to everything and spend as much time with each model as you can. What should you listen for? Here's how to evaluate a monitor:

    ■ **Listen for even frequency balance.** While listening to a piece of music that you know well, check to see whether any frequencies are exaggerated or attenuated. This is especially important in the midrange cross-over area (usually about 1.5 to 2.5 kHz). Listen especially to cymbals on the high end, vocals and guitars for the midrange, and bass and kick drum on the low end.

    ■ **Make sure the frequency balance stays the same at any level.** The less the frequency response changes as the level changes (especially when playing softly), the better. In other words, the speaker should have roughly the same frequency balance when the level is quiet as when it's loud.

    ■ **Make sure you have enough output level without distortion.** Be sure that there's enough clean level for your needs. Many powered monitors have built-in limiters that stop the speaker or amplifier from distorting, but they also may keep the system from getting as loud as you might need it to be.

Above all, don't buy a set of speakers without listening to them. It's usually very difficult for them to live up to your expectations if you've not heard them first. In fact, it's not a good idea to buy any speaker unless you're really in love with them. You'll have to listen to these monitors for many hours so you might as well like what you hear.

3. **Listen with source material that you know very well.** The only way to judge a monitor is to listen to material that you're very familiar with and have heard in a lot of different environments. This will give you the necessary reference point that you need to adequately judge what you're listening to. I like to use some things that I've recorded myself that I know inside and out and at least one favorite CD that I consider to be well recorded. Remember, no MP3s here. Use only CDs or a playback system with an even higher-quality 24-bit source, such as a personal digital recorder. That should give you some idea of the frequency response of the system.

Before the trend in monitors turned toward powered speakers, many engineers also brought their own amplifiers to the audition. This is because the amp/speaker combination is a delicate one, with each speaker having a much greater interdependence on the power source than most of us realize. In fact, the search for the perfect amplifier was almost as long suffering as the search for the perfect monitor. All of this has dwindled in recent years, thanks to monitors with built-in amplifiers perfectly matched to their speaker drivers by the manufacturer.

One of the things that I learned in my frequent speaker auditions for *EQ* magazine over the course of five years is that you can easily get used to just about any speaker if you use it enough and learn its strengths and weaknesses. It also helps to have a solid reference that you're sure of to compare the sound with. For instance, if you know how things sound in your car, then adjust your mixes so they work when you play them there.

Basic Monitor Setup

One thing frequently overlooked when auditioning or setting up near-field monitors is how the monitors are placed. This can make an enormous difference in the frequency balance and stereo field and should be addressed before you get into any serious listening. Here are a few things to experiment with before you settle on the exact placement.

■ **Check the distance between the monitors.** If the monitors are too close together, the stereo field will be smeared with no clear spatial definition. If the monitors are too far apart, the focal point or "sweet spot" will be too far behind you, and you'll hear the left or the right side but not both together. A rule of thumb is that the speakers should be as far apart as their distance from the listening position. That is, if you're 4 feet away from the monitors, then start by moving them 4 feet apart so that you make an equilateral triangle between you and the two monitors (see Figure 2.2). A simple tape measure will work fine to get it close. You can adjust them either in or out from there. That being said, there seems to be a magic distance that a lot of studio designers and room tuners like, and that's 67.5 inches between monitors—but that only works if you can sit roughly the same distance away from the monitors.

A really quick setup that we used to use in the days of consoles is to open your arms wide to each side and place the monitors at the tips of the fingers of each hand. This seemed to work well because of the built-in depth that the console would provide, but it doesn't really apply in these days of workstations where the monitors are a lot closer to you than ever. If that's the case, go back to the equilateral triangle outlined a moment ago.

■ **Check the angle of the monitors.** Improper angling will once again cause smearing of the stereo field, which causes a lack of instrument definition. The correct angle is determined strictly by taste, with some mixers preferring the monitors to be angled directly at their mixing position, while others prefer the focal point (the point where the sound from the tweeters converges) anywhere from 1 to 3 feet behind them to eliminate some of the "hype" of the speakers (if they have any) and widen the stereo field (see Figure 2.3).

To set the angle of the monitors, set up your monitors in the equilateral triangle fashion first, as described above. A great trick for getting excellent left/right imaging (both aural and visual, actually) is to mount a mirror over each tweeter and adjust the speakers so that your face is clearly seen in both mirrors at the same time when you are in your mixing position.

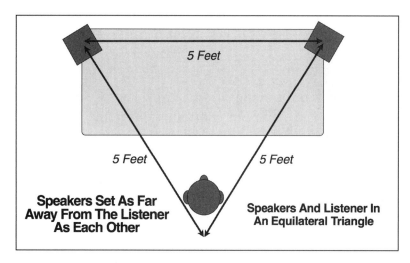

Figure 2.2 Speakers and listener in an equilateral triangle.

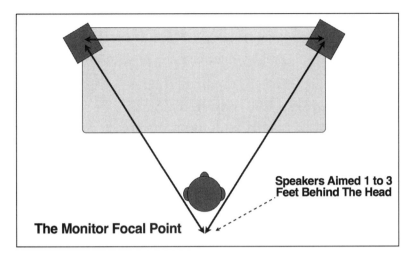

Figure 2.3 The monitor focal point.

■ **Check how the monitors are mounted.** Monitors that are mounted directly on top of a computer desk or console meter bridge without any decoupling (isolation) are subject to comb filter effects, especially in the low end. That is, the sound travels through the desk or console, through the floor, and reaches your ears first (because sound travels faster in denser material), before the direct sound from the monitors through the air gets there, causing phase cancellation. This can be more or less severe depending on whether the speakers are placed directly on the wood or mounted on a piece of carpet or similar material (very popular). The best way to decouple the monitors is to use the same method used when a commercial studio soffit-mounts its main monitors. Set the near-fields on a 1/2- or 3/4-inch piece of open cell neoprene, a thick mouse pad, or something like the Primacoustic Recoil Stabilizers (see Figure 2.4), and decoupling will no longer be an issue.

Figure 2.4 Recoil stabilizers.

Instead of mounting the near-fields on the desk or console, a better solution is to mount them on stands directly behind the meter bridge. Not only will this improve the low-frequency decoupling, but it will greatly decrease the unwanted reflections off the console.

- **Check how the monitor parameters are set.** With powered monitors, be sure that the parameter controls usually found on the rear of both monitors are set correctly for the application and are the same on each.

- **Check the position of the tweeters.** Many monitors are meant to be used in an upright position, yet users frequently will lay them down on their sides. This results in a variety of acoustic anomalies that deteriorate the sound. Most mixers prefer that the tweeters of a two- or three-way system be on the outside, thereby widening the stereo field. Occasionally, tweeters to the inside work, but this usually results in smearing of the stereo image. Experiment with both, however, because you never know.

- **Check the desk or console itself.** The angle of the desk or console; the type of materials used for the panels, knobs, and switches; the type of paint; and the size and composition of the armrest all make a difference in the sound due to reflections causing phase cancellation. If the sound of the near-fields on top of a desk or meter bridge is unacceptable, then try moving them toward you with extenders or put them on stands behind the console. (Don't forget to decouple them.)

How Loud (or Soft) Should I Listen?

One of the greatest misconceptions about music mixers (especially the great ones) is that they mix at high volume levels. In fact, quite the opposite is generally true. Most mixers find that they get better balances that translate well to the real listening world by monitoring at conversation level (79 dB SPL) or lower.

High SPL levels for long periods of time are generally not recommended for the following reasons:

- First the obvious one: Exposure to high volume levels for long periods of time may cause long-term physical damage.

- High volume levels for long periods of time will not only cause the onset of ear fatigue, but general physical fatigue as well. This means that you might effectively only be able to work 6 hours instead of the normal 8 (or 10 or 12) that's possible with lower levels.

- The ear has different frequency response curves at high volume levels that overcompensate on both the high and low frequencies. This means that your high-volume mix will generally sound pretty limp when played at softer levels.

■ Balances tend to blur at higher levels. What works at higher levels won't necessarily work when played softer. However, balances that are made at softer levels always work when played louder.

Now this isn't to say that all mixing should be done at the same level and everything should be played quietly. In fact, music mixers (as opposed to film, which always has a constant SPL level) tend to work at a variety of levels—up loud for a minute to check the low end and moderate while checking the EQ and effects. But the final balances usually will be done quietly.

Listening in Mono

Sooner or later, your mix will be played back in mono somewhere along the line, so it's best to check what will happen before you're surprised later. Listening in mono is a time-tested operation that gives the mixer the ability to check phase coherency, balances, and believe it or not, panning. Let's look at each one individually.

Phase Coherency

When a stereo mix is combined into mono, any elements that are out of phase will drop in level or even completely cancel out. This could be because the left and right outputs are wired out of phase (Pin 2 and Pin 3 of the XLR connector are reversed), which is the worst-case scenario, or perhaps because an out-of-phase effect causes the lead vocal or solo to disappear. In any event, it's prudent to listen in mono once in a while just to make sure that a mono disaster isn't lurking in the wings.

Balances

Many engineers listen to their mix in mono strictly to balance elements together, because they feel that they hear the balance better this way. Listening in mono is also a great way to tell when an element is masking another. As legendary engineer Andy Johns (Led Zeppelin, the Rolling Stones, Van Halen, Eric Clapton) once told me, "That used to be the big test [mixing in mono]. It was harder to do, and you had to be a bloody expert to make it work. In the old days we did mono mixes first and then did a quick one for stereo. We'd spend eight hours on the mono mix and half an hour on the stereo."

Panning

Although not many engineers are aware that their stereo panning can be improved while listening in mono, this is in fact a good way to achieve a level of precision not available in stereo. The late Don Smith (Rolling Stones, Stevie Nicks, Eurythmics) once said, "I check my panning in mono with one speaker, believe it or not. When you pan around in mono, all of a sudden you'll find the space for something that was masked before. If I want to find a place for the hi-hat, for instance, sometimes I'll go to mono and pan it around until all of a sudden, it's really present, and that's the spot. When you start to pan around in mono on all your drum mics, you'll hear all the phase come together. When you go to stereo, it makes things a lot better."

Listening Tips and Tricks

Most everyone wants to hear what their mix sounds like on different speakers and in different environments to get a more consumer-oriented perspective. There are some of the age-old standards, such as the car, a boom box, or listening down the hallway from the room you're mixing in.

These all work, but good television commercial producers use a similar technique that works equally well for music. Flip to a single small speaker (like an external computer speaker) in mono if possible, lower the volume so it's just perceptible, and see whether it still sounds like a record. Then raise the volume a tiny bit, walk out into the hall, and see whether you still like it. If it can pass this test, chances are the mix will fly just about anywhere it plays.

Listening on Several Systems

Most great mixers use at least a couple of systems to get a feel for how everything sounds—the main system where the mixer does all the major listening work and an alternate system for a check. The alternate system is usually one of somewhat lower quality that represents the lowest common denominator of what the average person might be listening on. Once upon a time, that meant a system like an Auratone (whose 5-inch driver represented what was commonly found on a typical television of the time), but today it's more often than not some sort of external computer speaker system.

The alternate speaker is used simply as a balance check to make sure that one of the instruments isn't either too loud or too soft in the mix. Also, one of the arts of mix balance is getting the kick drum and bass guitar to speak well on a small system, which is why an alternative monitor system is so important.

The Listening Environment

Probably the one area that gets overlooked in most home studios is the listening environment. While it's possible that you can get lucky with a great sound by just setting up a couple of near-field monitors in your room without thinking much about it, usually that's not the case, because normal garages, living rooms, and bedrooms aren't intended as listening spaces and have little in the way of acoustic treatment.

Potential Acoustic Problems

Although an in-depth discussion of acoustic treatment is beyond the scope of this book, here are a few things to avoid if you can help it.

1.   **Avoid placing speakers up against a wall.** This usually results in some strong peaks in the low-frequency response. The farther away you can get from the wall, the less it influences the frequency response of your monitors, and the smoother that response will be.

2. **Avoid the corners of the room.** Worse than the wall is a corner, because it will reinforce the low end even more than when placed against a wall. Even worse than that is if only one speaker is in the corner, which will cause the response of your system to be lopsided.

3. **Avoid being closer to one wall of the room than the other.** If one speaker is closer to a side wall than the other, once again you'll get a totally different frequency response between the two because of phase issues. It's best to set up directly in the center of the room if possible.

4. **Avoid different types of wall absorption.** If one side of the room contains a window and the other is painted drywall or something like carpet or Sonex, once again you'll have an unbalanced stereo image, because one side is brighter than the other. Try to make the walls on each side of the speakers the same in terms of absorption quality.

ARC

Of course, the real world of home studios means there's never an ideal solution, and usually at least one of the aforementioned four issues occurs. Luckily, T-RackS 3 has an add-on called the *Advanced Room Correction* system, or ARC (see Figure 2.5), that's a plug-in that measures the frequency response of your room and then provides a software equalization solution to eliminate those nasty peaks and valleys caused by a less than ideal listening environment. As you're probably already aware, professional acoustic treatment, measurement, and equalization is expensive and may not even be possible for your environment, but ARC is an inexpensive solution that has the advantage of being usable in any environment (unlike acoustic treatment, which needs to be customized).

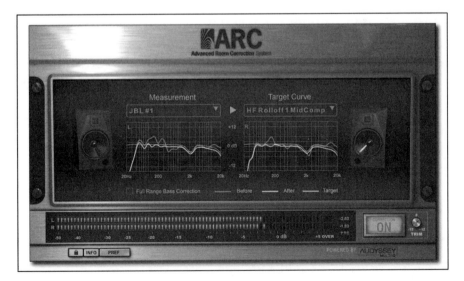

Figure 2.5 Advanced Room Correction system.

ARC consists of a calibrated measurement microphone and the software plug-in for either T-RackS 3 or your favorite DAW. ARC will measure your room, show you the response, and then correct it and show you the curve as soon as you select Correction On. In five guided steps, ARC can take you from a room full of sonic horrors to one where you can finally hear all the sonic details of your mix. Unlike correction systems built into some popular monitors, ARC covers the entire frequency spectrum and allows you to develop a listening curve for the entire room, not only at the engineer's sweet spot, so your clients can hear just what you're hearing.

ARC is self-guided and comes with a pretty thorough instruction manual, but here are a number of points to keep in mind.

- The more measurements you take, the more likely the problems in your room will be corrected.

- The measurement microphone requires 48-volt phantom power to operate.

- Any noise or movement that you make during a measurement could invalidate the measurement, and you'll have to start over.

- Any changes in the room (such as a large object brought in or removed or a piece of furniture or gear moved to a different location) means that the environment requires a new measurement.

- Because the nasty peaks in the bass response have been smoothed out, it will take some time to get used to the response, so don't make an immediate judgment after the measurement and correction.

- If ARC is used as a plug-in on your stereo buss, then it must be removed during export, or your mix will permanently contain the ARC EQ. ARC is meant for monitoring only.

- You can use the measurement microphone that comes with ARC just as you would any other microphone for recording instruments, amplifiers, or vocals. It is an omni microphone, though, so it might seem a little bass-light compared to other microphones in your collection that have a directional pattern, which results in a low-end boost because of the proximity effect.

Summary Questions

You can find answers to the Summary Questions in the Appendix at the end of this book.

1. What are three reasons why the monitor speakers that your favorite mixer uses might not work for you?

2. How do you evaluate a monitor?

3.   How far apart should the speakers be placed?

4.   What happens if they're too close together? Too far apart?

5.   What is the monitor focal point?

6.   Why is it located at a point just behind the mixer's head?

7.   Why is decoupling the monitors so important?

8.   What are two ways to decouple monitors?

9.   Why is sustained listening at high volume levels not recommended?

10.   Why is a lot of mixing done at quiet levels?

3 Using T-RackS Dynamics during Mixing

All the processor modules in T-RackS 3 can be used as plug-ins for just about any currently available DAW software package that can support VST, RTAS, or Audio Unit formats (which is almost all of them). This gives you the possibility of using the processors on individual tracks, subgroups, or the stereo buss (which we'll cover in Chapter 5, "Mix Buss Compression"). Let's take a look at some of the processors and their application on individual tracks.

Compressors

The dynamics of music have always had to be controlled in order to convert the naturally large dynamic range of organic sound into a rather small artificial dynamic range that fits on a distribution medium such as magnetic tape or a vinyl record. As the distribution became more modern with the introduction of the CD and now online audio files, dynamic control used specifically for the medium wasn't needed in quite the same way anymore, but everyone liked the sound so much that more sophisticated control of dynamics became the norm. In fact, dynamics control like compression has become so important that it can be said that the use of compression is the single most vital element of making a recording sound professional.

A Brief Explanation

A compressor is an automated level control that uses the input signal to determine the output level. The Ratio parameter controls the amount that the output level from the compressor will increase compared to the input level. For instance, if the compression ratio is 4:1 (four to one), for every 4 dB of level that goes into the compressor, only 1 dB will come out once the signal reaches the threshold level (the point at which the compressor begins to work). If a gain ratio is set at 8:1, then for every 8 dB that goes into the unit, only 1 dB will come out of the output. Some compressors have a fixed ratio, but the parameter is variable on most units from 1:1 (no compression) to as much as 100:1 (which makes it a limiter, a process that we'll tackle later in this chapter). A Threshold control sets the input level point where the compression will kick in. Below that point, there is no compression.

Most compressors have Attack and Release parameters. These controls determine how fast or slow the compressor reacts to the beginning (attack) and end (release) of the signal envelope. Many compressors have an Auto mode that automatically sets the attack and release according to the dynamics of the signal. Although Auto works relatively well, it still doesn't allow for the precise settings required by certain source material. Some compressors (like the Vintage 670) have a fixed attack and release (the 670 has five fixed selections), which helps give the compressor a distinctive sound.

When a compressor actually compresses the signal, the level is decreased, so there is another control called Make-Up Gain or Output that allows the signal to be boosted back up to its original level or beyond.

Compression to Control Dynamics

Controlling dynamics means keeping the level of the sound even. In other words, it refers to lifting the level of the soft passages and lowering the level of the loud ones so that there's less of a difference between them. Anywhere from 2 to 6 dB or so at a 2:1 to 8:1 ratio is usually used to keep the dynamics of the signal under control, although some situations may require more.

Here are a few instances where controlling dynamics is useful:

- **On a bass guitar.** Most basses inherently have notes that are louder or softer than others, depending upon where they're played on the neck of the instrument. Compression (a few dB at a 4:1 or 8:1 ratio) evens out these differences.

- **On a lead vocal.** Most singers can't sing every word or line at the same level, so some words get buried as a result. Compression evens out the level differences so you can better hear every word. The amount of compression can vary wildly on a vocal if it has a lot of dynamic range—say, from a whisper to a scream within the same song—so it's not uncommon to have as much as 10 dB or even more in those types of situations.

- **On a kick or snare drum.** Sometimes a drummer doesn't hit every beat with the same intensity, which makes the pulse of the song erratic. Compression can make all the hits have the same intensity. Once again, a few dB at a 4:1 or 8:1 ratio does the trick.

Compression as an Effect

Compression can radically change the sound of a track. A track that is compressed with the right kind of compressor and with the right settings for the program can seem closer to the listener and can seem more aggressive and exciting. With the Attack and Release controls, you can modify the volume envelope of a sound to have more or less attack, which can make it sound punchy or fatter. Surprisingly, this can mean using massive amounts of compression (like 15 or 20 dB) or hardly any at all (a single dB) because of the inherent sound of a particular processor. Many engineers just like what it sounds like with a compressor in the signal chain with little to no compression, but you have to have some big ears to tell the difference sometimes.

Amount of Compression

The amount of compression you add is usually to taste, but generally speaking, the more compression, the greater the effect. Less compression (6 dB or less) is more for controlling dynamics than for the sonic quality, but it's common to see radical amounts of compression used, with as much as 15 or 20 dB routinely used for electric guitars, room mics, drums, and even vocals. As with almost everything else, the amount of compression depends on the song, the arrangement, the player, the room, the instrument or vocalist, or the sound you're looking for.

Setting the Compressor

Because the timing of the attack and release is so important, here are a few steps to help you set up the compressor. Assuming that you have some kind of constant tempo in the song, you can use the snare drum to set up the attack and release parameters. This method also works for other instruments in the same manner.

1. Start with the slowest attack and fastest release settings on the compressor.

2. Turn the attack faster until the instrument (in this case, the snare) begins to dull. Stop at that point.

3. Adjust the release time so that after the snare hit, the volume goes back to 90 to 100 percent of normal by the next snare beat.

4. Add the rest of the mix back in and listen. Make slight adjustments to the attack and release times as needed.

The idea is to make the compressor breathe in time with the song.

Compressor Modules

T-RackS 3 Deluxe features three compressor modules, each with its own sonic characteristics.

Vintage Tube Model 670

The Vintage Tube Model 670 compressor sounds good on just about anything you want to use it on (see Figure 3.1). It provides an intangible "glue" to the track even if the gain reduction meter is hardly registering due to its built-in coloration, which can be increased or decreased by the Input settings. That being said, try it on vocals, bass, or any kind of guitar using 5 or 6 dB of gain reduction and a Time Constant set on 1. It won't sound too compressed, yet the result will be consistent and solid. Keep the Threshold controls low (2 or 3) when you want the compression to sound its most transparent. Set it high (anything over 5) when you really want it noticeable.

Figure 3.1   The Vintage Tube Model 670.

The 670 sounds great on a drum submix. You may only need a few dB (or a lot more), but it will pull the sound together, cover the inconsistencies, and bring the kit right up in your face. Depending upon the pulse of the song, you might want to try different Time Constant selections, with 5 or 6 usually working well. Another interesting feature is the Lat/Vert mode, where the left channel is routed to the center (the M or mono), and the right channel is routed to the side (the S). This allows you to compress the center and the sides of the stereo program independently. You can get some interesting sounds this way and carve out a section of your mix so other instruments can sit better.

Table 3.1 Starting Settings for the Vintage 670

Parameter	Setting
AGC	Link
Left-Right Time Constant	1
Left-Right Input Gain	Set to register 2 dB of gain reduction
Left-Right Time Threshold	3
Level	0 dB

- Increase the Left and Right Time Constant controls to adjust the release times.

- Increase the Left and Right Threshold controls to make the compression sound more aggressive.

Opto Compressor

The Opto Compressor (see Figure 3.2) gets its name for emulating a compressor like the famed LA-2A that uses an electro-optical element to control the amount of compression applied. The sound of the Opto varies from that of a traditional hardware-based optical compressor in that it was built for clean, transparent sound, while the hardware

Figure 3.2 The Opto Compressor.

versions are colored. What is the same is the gradual release curve that's both gentle and musical.

You'll find that the Opto Compressor works great on vocals, bass, and even drums because of its sonic characteristics. Start with the Attack and Release controls at the mid position and the Ratio at 2:1, but don't be afraid to use the high ratios (10:1 and higher) for a more dramatic effect. The Compression control acts like a Threshold control, with more compression occurring as you turn the control clockwise.

Keep in the mind that at low ratios (such as 2:1), the maximum amount of compression might only be 3 or 4 dB, which is normal for this type of compressor. For more compression, increase the Ratio control.

Table 3.2 Starting Settings for the Opto Compressor

Parameter	Setting
Attack	50 ms
Release	30 ms
Ratio	3:1
Compression	5
Input	0 dB

- Decrease the Attack time to catch the transients.

- Increase the Release time to breathe with the track or smooth the sound of the compression.

- Increase the Compression control to increase the compression.

Classic Tube Compressor

The Classic Tube Compressor is an emulation of a typical early tube-based hardware compressor that was built back in the days when extreme parameter settings weren't a priority. Its maximum gain reduction ratio is only a little under 5:1, but it's surprising how good it sounds on just about anything at 1.5:1. Like most things built around tubes, it has a rather slow attack time that can be useful on transient material like drums, even when turned fully counterclockwise. The Input Drive control acts like a Threshold control.

The Classic Tube Compressor has a couple of neat features that you don't find on other compressors (see Figure 3.3). The first is a Sidechain High-Pass Filter control, which allows the compressor to work only on the frequencies that are above what's selected by the control. In other words, if the Sidechain HPF control reads 76.4 Hz, that means only the frequencies above 76.4 will be acted on by the Classic Tube Compressor, and the frequencies below will not.

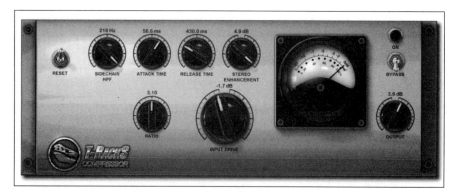

Figure 3.3   The Classic Tube Compressor.

What this will effectively do is boost the low end, since it's not being compressed much, but be careful that it doesn't get too big if you use it set beyond 100 Hz.

Another interesting parameter that's unique to this processor is the Stereo Enhancement control, which affects the imaging of a stereo track. Turning it up will increase the stereo width, and turning it down (below 0 dB) will contract it. This works great if a track seems just a little too down the middle and needs a little width. Keep your eye on the Phase Correlation meter in the meter section as you add width, to make sure that everything stays mono compatible.

The Classic Tube Compressor is pretty much an all-purpose unit in that it works great on drums (try it on 1.5:1 with 5 or 6 dB of gain reduction), bass, piano, acoustic and electric guitars, loops, and synths. It won't give you anything radical, but you can always count on its great sonic quality.

Table 3.3 Starting Settings for the Classic Tube Compressor

Parameter	Setting
Sidechain HPF	32 Hz
Attack Time	82 ms
Release Time	29 ms
Ratio	3:1
Input Drive	0 dB
Stereo Enhancement	0 dB

- Increase the Input Drive to increase the amount of compression.

- Increase the Stereo Enhancement control to widen the stereo field.

- Decrease the Attack time to catch the transients.

- Increase the Release time to breathe with the track or smooth the sound of the compression.

- Increase the Sidechain HPF to increase the low-end response.

Limiters

A compressor can sometimes be adjusted to work as a limiter, or more often the limiter is a dedicated unit. Any time the compression ratio is set to 10:1 or more, the result is considered limiting. A limiter is essentially a brick wall for level, allowing the signal to get only to a certain point and little more. Think of it like a governor that's sometimes used on trucks to make sure that they don't go over the speed limit. After you hit 65 mph (or whatever the speed limit in your state is), no matter how much more you press the gas pedal, you won't go faster. It's the same with a limiter. When you hit the pre-determined level, no matter how much you try to go beyond it, the level pretty much stays the same.

Limiters are found everywhere in the audio business—from live sound, where they're used to keep the level from going so loud that it pops the speakers or the eardrum of a singer with in-ear monitors; to the end of a signal chain of a radio or television station, where the FCC demands that it broadcast at 50,000 watts and not a fraction more; to the mastering signal chain, where an overload can cause some nasty digital distortion or a vinyl record to skip. (We'll talk more about mastering in Chapters 7 through 12.)

During tracking and mixing, limiters aren't used as much as compressors, but they are used in instances where an instrument has a lot of transient spikes, such as a thumb-slapped bass.

Limiter Modules

T-RackS 3 Deluxe features three limiter modules, each with its own sonic characteristics and uses.

Brickwall Limiter

One of the things that the Brickwall Limiter (see Figure 3.4) excels at is pulling the ambience out of a drum track. By squashing the track hard, the ambience rises in level along with the punch of the drums. This works great on a stereo drum loop or across the submaster buss of a drum kit.

Figure 3.4   The Brickwall Limiter.

Set the Ceiling control at about −0.1 dB and raise the Input control until the Gain Reduction meter reads −8 or −10 dB. Set the Style selector for any of the Advanced or Saturation selections, the Attack control fully to the right, and the Release control fully to the left. You can control the amount of ambience with the Release control. A shorter release makes the ambience pop, while a longer release retains more of the original direct/ambience ratio.

Table 3.4 Starting Settings for the Brickwall Limiter

Parameter	Setting
Input	0 dB
Attack Time	1 ms
Release Time	60 ms
Style	Clean
Output Ceiling	−0.1 dB

- Increase the Input so the Gain Reduction meter peaks at −3 to −6 dB.

- Decrease the Attack Time to catch the transients to prevent overload.

- Increase the Release Time to breathe with the track or smooth the sound of the compression.

Classic Clipper

The Classic Clipper is another great plug-in for drums (see Figure 3.5). It's simple and very punchy. Increase the Gain until the Gain Reduction meter reads around −8 or −10 dB. Set the Output to −1 dB and start with the Slope control all the way to the left. This should give you a great, punchy drum track with a fair amount of ambience without much work at all, since the clipping is soft and produces a bit of a "saturation" effect. As you move the Slope control clockwise, you'll find that the drums begin to sound punchier as the saturation effect is decreased. Be careful with increasing the Slope control too much, though, because the drums will begin to sound choked at some point.

Figure 3.5   The Classic Clipper.

Table 3.5 Starting Settings for the Classic Clipper	
Parameter	**Setting**
Gain	0 dB
Slope	−12 dB
Output	−1 dB

■ Increase the Gain control until the desired amount of gain reduction is achieved on the Gain Reduction meter.

■ Increase the Slope control to increase the amount of aggression characteristic in the compression.

Multiband Limiter

The Multiband Limiter is unique in that it will shape the timbre of an instrument in ways that an EQ just can't touch (see Figure 3.6). By raising or lowering the Level control of each band and then adjusting the Crossover controls, the tonal quality of the instrument will change in a way similar to an EQ, but only that particular band will be compressed.

Figure 3.6   The Multiband Limiter.

For instance, if you wanted just to tighten up the low end, you'd increase the level of the low-frequency band while adjusting the low/mid frequency Crossover control to focus in on the exact frequencies that you want to affect. This works great on unruly drum kits, bass, acoustic guitar, and piano.

The presets are a good place to start, but don't be afraid to increase the Input Drive and Overload controls as needed.

Table 3.6 Starting Settings for the Multiband Limiter

Parameter	Setting
Band Threshold	0 dB
Band Level	0 dB
Crossover	200 Hz and 7.5 kHz
Input Drive	3.5
Release Time	80 ms
Overload	0 dB

- Decrease the Band Threshold controls to increase the compression of that particular band.

- Increase the Input Drive to increase the compression of all bands at the same time.

- Increase the Release Time to breathe with the track or smooth the sound of the compression.

- Increase the Overload control to increase the loudness.

De-Essers

Sometimes compressing a vocal that's been heavily EQed (or EQing a vocal that's been heavily compressed) results in short bursts of high-frequency energy where the S's are overemphasized. This is known as *sibilance,* and it varies from annoying to undesirable. A special type of compressor that can be tuned to compress only between 3 and 10 kHz to eliminate sibilance is called a *de-esser.*

Although T-RackS doesn't currently include a de-esser module at the time of this writing, IK Multimedia has announced that one is being developed and will be released in the future. In the meantime, there are two global presets for de-essing that utilize the parallel chain (De-Ess Master 1 and 2). There are also two ways to manually overcome sibilance.

■ Cut the sibilant sections from the track and paste them on a second track. Insert the Vintage 670 compressor in the second sibilant track and set it to very fast attack and release (Time Constant 1) and the threshold to trigger on every sibilant part. The compressor will now act as a de-esser.

■ Although not as precise as the preceding method, you can also use the Multiband Limiter as a de-esser. Set it so the high-frequency band is the only one to trigger to help eliminate sibilants.

Table 3.7 Multiband Limiter Settings for De-Essing

Parameter	Setting
Crossover	3.5 to 7 kHz
Release Time	80 ms
Overload	−5.3
Input Drive	3
Level	0 dB
Threshold	−1 to −10 dB

Summary Questions

You can find answers to the Summary Questions in the Appendix at the end of this book.

1. What does a compressor do?

2. What does a gain ratio of 6:1 mean?

3. Give two situations where you might use a compressor.

4. What can happen if you set the attack of a compressor too fast?

5. What can happen if you set the release of a compressor too fast?

6. Describe how to set up a compressor.

7. What's the difference between a compressor and a limiter?

8. At what compression ratio does a compressor become a limiter?

9. List three instances where a limiter would be used instead of a compressor.

10. At what level is the Output Ceiling control usually set on the Brickwall Limiter?

4 Using the T-RackS EQ and Metering during Mixing

T-RackS 3 has several powerful equalizers available as plug-ins during mixing. Before we discuss them specifically, let's take a look at how equalizers work and how they're used.

Equalizers

Even though most engineers try to make their tracks sound as big and as clear as possible during tracking and overdubs, the total frequency range of some or all of the tracks is often still somewhat limited when it comes time to mix. This could be because the tracks were recorded in a different studio using different monitors, a different signal path was used during recording, or the tonal quality of an instrument was limited. As a result, the mixing engineer must extend the frequency range of those tracks.

In the quest to make things sound bigger, fatter, brighter, and clearer, the equalizer is the chief tool that most mixers use. But perhaps more than any other audio tool, the use of the equalizer requires a special kind of skill.

What Are You Trying to Do?

There are three primary goals when equalizing. You're trying to:

- Make an instrument sound clearer and more defined.

- Make the instrument or mix bigger and larger than life.

- Make all the elements of a mix fit together better by juggling frequencies so that each instrument has its own predominant frequency range.

A Description of the Audio Spectrum

Before we examine some methods of equalizing, it's important to note the areas of the audio band and the effect they have on what we hear. We can break down the audio band into six distinct ranges, each one having an enormous impact on the total sound.

Frequency Band	Description	Consequences
Sub-Bass16 Hz to 60 Hz	Encompasses sounds that are often felt more than heard and give the music a sense of power.	Too much emphasis in this range makes the music sound muddy. Attenuating this range (especially below 40 Hz) can clean up a mix considerably.
Bass 60 Hz to 250 Hz	Contains the fundamental notes of the rhythm section.	EQing this range can change the musical balance, making it fat or thin. Too much boost in this range can make the music sound boomy.
Low Mids250 Hz to 2 kHz	Contains the low-order harmonics of most musical instruments.	Can introduce a telephone-like quality to the music if boosted too much. Boosting the 500- to 1,000-Hz octave makes the instruments sound horn-like. Boosting the 1- to 2-kHz octave makes them sound tinny. Excess output in this range can cause listening fatigue.
High Mids 2 to 4 kHz	Controls the speech recognition sounds of m, b, and v.	Too much boost in this range, especially at 3 kHz, can introduce a lisping quality to a voice. Too much boost in this range can cause listening fatigue. Dipping the 3-kHz range on instrument backgrounds and slightly peaking 3 kHz on vocals can make the vocals audible without having to decrease the instrumental level in mixes where the voice would otherwise seem buried.
Presence 4 to 6 kHz	Is responsible for the clarity and definition of voices and instruments.	Boosting this range can make the music seem closer to the listener. Reducing the 5-kHz content of a mix makes the sound more distant and transparent.
Brilliance 6 to 16 kHz	Controls the brilliance and clarity of sounds.	Too much emphasis in this range can produce sibilance on the vocals.

Using the Equalizer

Before you touch an equalizer, keep in mind that there are two principles that will help you.

- The fewer instruments that are in the mix, the bigger each one should sound.

- Conversely, the more instruments in the mix, the smaller each one needs to be for everything to fit together.

Subtractive Equalization

One of the best ways to equalize is by attenuating frequencies instead of boosting them. This is what's known as *subtractive equalization*. It's a favorite of experienced engineers because the sound of the track is more natural than if you boosted frequencies, because of the lack of phase shift that's induced. Every time that you boost an EQ, there's an amount of phase shift that's added to the signal as a byproduct of the way an electronic equalizer works. (The Linear Phase Equalizer sounds so good because the phase shift is minimized.) The more EQ that's added, the more phase shift that's induced. The phase shift is a form of distortion that makes the EQed track more difficult to blend with the others. That's why subtractive equalization is so powerful—because no phase shift is induced by cutting a frequency, so the track is better able to blend with the others as a result.

Here's how subtractive equalization works:

1. Set the Boost/Cut control to a moderate level of cut. (Eight or 10 dB should work.)

2. Sweep through the frequencies until you find the frequency where the sound has the least amount of boxiness and the most definition.

3. Adjust the amount of cut to taste. Be aware that too much cut makes the sound thinner.

There are two spots in the frequency spectrum where the subtractive equalization is particularly effective—between 400 and 600 Hz and between 2 and 4 kHz. This is because most directional microphones provide a natural boost at 400 to 600 Hz because of the proximity effect brought about by close-miking, and many mics (especially those known for being good vocal mics) have a presence boost between 2 and 4 kHz. Dipping those frequencies a few dB (more or less as needed) can make the track much more natural than if you were to try to add frequencies instead.

If you're using a limited number of microphones (or even just one) to record all the instruments in a home studio, these two frequency bands (or any other where there's a peak in the response) will build up as more and more instruments are added. By dipping those frequency bands a bit, you'll find that all the instruments sit a lot better in the mix without having to add much EQ at all.

Easy-to-Remember Golden Rules of Equalization

- If it sounds muddy, cut some at 250 Hz.

- If it sounds honky, cut some at 500 Hz.

- Cut if you're trying to make things sound clearer.

- Boost if you're trying to make things sound different.

- You can't boost something that's not there in the first place.

Juggling Frequencies

Most veteran engineers know that soloing an instrument and equalizing it without hearing the other instruments will probably start making you chase your tail as you make each instrument bigger and brighter sounding. In no time, the instruments begin to conflict with each other frequency-wise. That's why it's important to listen to other instruments while you're EQing; they'll fit together better by juggling frequencies so that each instrument has its own predominant frequency range. Here's how it's done.

1.   Start with the rhythm section (bass and drums). The bass should be clear and distinct when played against the drums, especially the kick and snare.

     You should be able to hear each instrument distinctly. If not, do the following:

     - Make sure that no two equalizers are boosting at the same frequency. If they are, move one to a slightly higher or lower frequency.

     - If an instrument is cut at a certain frequency, boost the frequency of the other instrument at that same frequency. For example, if the kick is cut at 500 Hz, boost the bass at 500 Hz.

2.   Add the next most predominant element—usually the vocal—and proceed as above.

3.   Add the rest of the elements into the mix one by one. As you add each instrument, check it against the previous elements, as above.

Remember:

- The idea is to hear each instrument clearly, and the best way for that to happen is for each instrument to live in its own frequency band.

- After frequency juggling, an instrument might sound terrible when soloed by itself. That's okay. The idea is for it to work in the track.

■ You probably will have to EQ in a circle, where you start with one instrument, tweak another that's clashing, return to the original one, and then go back again over and over until you achieve the desired separation.

The Magic High-Pass Filter

One of the most useful and overlooked processors in a mixer's toolkit is the high-pass filter. The low frequencies of many instruments just get in the way of each other and don't add much to the sound. That's why if you roll the low frequencies off below 150 or 200 Hz on instruments other than the kick and bass, the mix begins to clean up almost magically. Rolling off the low frequencies of a vocal mic can eliminate the rumble of trucks and machinery that you can't hear anyway because they're so low, yet muddy up the mix. Even rolling off the bass and drums at between 40 and 60 Hz can sometimes make the mix a lot louder and punchier without affecting the low end much.

EQ Modules

T-RackS 3 has three different equalizer modules, each with a different sonic characteristic. Let's take a look.

The Classic Equalizer

If you take notice, most recording consoles have a high-pass filter built into the EQ section; but when we're mixing in the box, we have to resort to plug-ins for a high-pass filter. The Classic Equalizer works great for this application because it has a built-in high-pass filter on its lowest band (see Figure 4.1). Set the frequency for between 40 and 60 Hz on instruments such as bass and drums and higher (150 to 250 Hz) for other instruments to eliminate some of the low frequencies that don't add much to the sound and to make them fit better in the mix.

Figure 4.1 The Classic Equalizer.

The Classic Equalizer has a familiar feel to it because it's just like the equalizer found on most recording consoles, with shelving-type equalizers on the low and high ends and two bands of parametric equalizers in the middle. Add a low-pass filter to go along with the high-pass, and you have a powerful six-band equalizer that can handle most equalization jobs with little effort.

The Classic EQ also has an M/S matrix mode that allows you to equalize more on the sides of a stereo image rather than in the middle or vice versa, as with most equalizers. Make sure you try this mode, as it can carve out a space without resorting to excessive equalization.

The Linear Phase Equalizer

The Linear Phase EQ (see Figure 4.2) is used when you want nice, clean, uncolored equalization even with radical amounts applied. The LPEQ is unique in that it has six bands of EQ, which is more than you'll usually find on most EQs. It works great on natural acoustic instruments, such as piano and acoustic guitar, and it's dynamite on vocals because of its lack of audible side effects.

Figure 4.2 The Linear Phase Equalizer.

Yet another trick that's common to many of the processors in T-RackS 3 is the M/S mode, which is entered by selecting the button on the top left of the processor. The M/S mode uses a Mid-Side matrix that allows you to select where the process works in the stereo image. The M assigns the process to the center of the stereo image, as usual, but the S (or side) makes it seem as if the equalization is occurring at the outside edges of the stereo spectrum. Most of the time you'll find that the Mid mode works best, but occasionally the Side mode will allow you to add EQ in a way that works better, such as brightening up a track without affecting a lead vocal.

Tube Program Equalizer EQP-1A

The original Pultec EQP-1A hardware EQ is a totally unique equalizer, and nothing really sounds like it (see Figure 4.3), because its vacuum tube circuitry was designed in the early days of audio, when the needs of the engineers were a lot less sophisticated.

The sound of the EQP-1A is just so unique; the highs shimmer, the lows are round, and the mids are smooth. The analog version of the EQP-1A was always difficult to find, as there are so few of them left; but luckily, IK Multimedia has made it available without any of the analog heartaches that come along with a hardware unit (like being noisy because of old tubes and components).

Figure 4.3   The EQP-1A Tube Program Equalizer.

The EQP-1A is interesting in that it has both Boost and Atten (attenuation) controls, but they're not at the same frequency, so they don't cancel out like with other equalizers. As a result, sometimes you can more easily get the sound you're looking for by using both the Boost and Atten controls at the same time.

As with all T-RackS processor modules, don't be afraid to try the M/S function to EQ the sides rather than the middle. It can really make an instrument sound great sometimes and carve out a space in the mix not possible otherwise.

Metering

The superb T-RackS 3 meter array is also available as a plug-in (see Figure 4.4) and provides a variety of features, including a precision peak meter, an RMS meter, a loudness meter, a phase correlation meter, and a spectrum analyzer. (See Chapter 9, "Metering," for a full explanation of each one.)

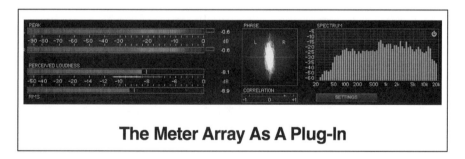

Figure 4.4   The Meter Array.

Even though every DAW has peak meters available on every channel, the precision and variety of the T-RackS metering can become invaluable in many situations. Let's take a look at some scenarios.

■ Before you EQ a track, you can take a look at the Spectrum Analyzer to see whether there are any outstanding peaks or dips in the response that require your attention.

■ To set the buss compression of a drum kit so it's more "in your face," you can take a look at the Loudness meter to guide you on the amount of compression to apply.

■ You can set the amount of compression during tracking or mixing by looking at the precision Peak meter and the RMS meter. You can see the overall level increase as the peaks come under control.

■ For anything recorded in stereo that doesn't sound quite right, such as piano, drum overheads, toms, or room mics, you can check the Phase Correlation meter to see whether there's a phase problem in your miking.

■ On the stereo buss (which we'll discuss more in Chapter 5, "Mix Buss Compression"), you can check the mix for frequency peaks or deficiencies with the Spectrum Analyzer, set the buss compression level with the Peak and RMS meters, and check the phase with the Phase Correlation meter.

Using the Spectrum Analyzer during Mixing

The Spectrum Analyzer is a particularly effective part of the metering package to help you find frequencies that muddy things up yet don't add much to the mix. Here's how to use it.

1. Solo the bass. If you see any energy at 20 Hz, insert a high-pass filter and eliminate it. Energy at this frequency can't be heard and just makes things muddy.

2. Solo the kick and repeat the process. Usually either the kick or the bass occupies the lower frequency bands at 40 and 60 Hz, but not both, as they'll fight for attention. Attenuate that area for one or the other depending upon the song.

3. Solo the other tracks one at a time. Take a look to see what kind of energy is below 150 Hz or so. The kick and bass already contain energy in these bands, so you can insert your HPF and attenuate that area on the track to clean things up.

The T-RackS metering package is a great plug-in that can provide signal intelligence that you can't get any other way as easily. Don't overlook it.

Summary Questions

You can find answers to the Summary Questions in the Appendix at the end of this book.

1. What are the primary goals of equalizing?

2. What are the six major frequency bands?

3. Which frequency band can cause listener fatigue if emphasized too much?

4. Which frequency band can cause the "m," "b," and "v" voice sounds to be masked if emphasized too much?

5. Which frequency band can cause the music to seem closer to the listener when boosted?

6. Which frequency band can cause vocal sibilance if emphasized too much?

7. The more instruments in the mix, the _____ each has to be for everything to fit together.

8. What is subtractive equalization?

9. Why is subtractive equalization used?

10. Where are the two spots in the frequency spectrum that subtractive equalization is most effective?

5 Mix Buss Compression

Along with compressing the individual track of a song, many engineers place a stereo compressor across the mix buss to affect the entire mix as well. Originally this came about when artists began asking why their mixes sounded different in the studio from what they heard on the radio or when their record came from the pressing plant. (It was still vinyl in those days.) Indeed, both the radio and the record did sound different because an additional round (or two) of compression was added in both mastering and broadcast. To simulate what this would sound like, mixing engineers began to add a touch of compression across the mix buss. The problem was, everybody liked the sound so much that now the majority of records have at least a bit (a few dB) of compression added to the stereo mix despite the fact that it will probably be re-compressed again at mastering and yet again if played on the radio or television.

Why Use Buss Compression?

Generally, you'll find that most renowned mixers use the buss compressor to add a sort of "glue" to the track so the instruments fit together better, but that also means that they'll actually use very little compression. In fact, sometimes only a dB or two of gain reduction at the most is added for the final mix. That being said, many mixers will also offer their clients (artists, band members, producers, and label execs) a more compressed version to simulate what it will sound like after it's mastered. This "client mix" is achieved by using a signal path across the mix buss that's similar to what a mastering engineer would use—that is, a compressor that's fed into a limiter at the end of the chain to raise the level to a point similar to a mastered release (see Figure 5.1).

Because the clients get used to hearing the "client mix," it's so easy to let buss compression get out of hand. One of the problems with compressing too much is that it leaves the mastering engineer a lot less room to work, and in the case of a track that's hyper-compressed, it virtually eliminates the ability for the mastering engineer to be of much help at all. See Chapter 10, "Mastering 101 (The Mastering Process)."

When to Use It

There are two times during the mix that you can insert your buss compression—when you first start the mix or toward completion. Although the two choices might not seem all that different, you will get a slightly different result from each.

Figure 5.1   Mix buss signal path for a client mix.

At the End of the Mix

If you wait to insert the buss compressor later in the mix (the way it has been tradi-
tionally done), the compressor settings will be a little less aggressive, since you've
probably already inserted a pretty good amount of compression on the individual
tracks. Usually it's inserted at the point during the mix where most of your elements and
effects have already been added to your mix and it's now time to concentrate on balances. One of the advantages of inserting buss compression toward the end is that if you
don't like the sound, you can easily substitute a different compressor or even eliminate it
altogether. It doesn't take much (usually a dB or two) to make a sonic difference to
where it's at least a little bigger sounding.

At the Beginning of the Mix

The other way is to insert the buss compressor right at the start of the mix and build
your mix into it. Because this affects the dynamics of the mix right from the beginning,
mixing this way might take a little getting used to, but it has some advantages. First, the
mix comes together a little more quickly, since it has that "glue" almost right away as a
result.

Second, you'll find yourself using a little less compression on the individual tracks. This
has the secondary benefit of giving you greater control of the overall compression of the
mix. If you feel like there's too much, it's pretty easy to back off on the buss compressor

to where you or your client feels better about it (if that's what they're looking for); whereas if you added it toward the end, sometimes the only way to dial it back is to tweak the individual instrument compression, which can take quite a bit of time and rebalancing.

The third thing is that the buss compressor tends to even out the levels of the individual instruments a lot, so you need less automation. The downside of doing it this way is that if you decide you don't like the sound of the compressor, the overall sound and balance of the mix can change a lot when you insert a different one. When starting with the buss compressor in the signal path from the beginning of the mix, you'll find that you'll be using somewhat more compression—about 3 or 4 dB.

Mix Buss Compressor Alternatives

If you don't like the sound of a mix buss compressor or you don't feel like you have enough control, there is an alternative—compress the subgroups instead. This means that you break the individual elements into their own subgroups, such as drums and bass (the rhythm section), guitars, keyboards, and vocals. An even simpler configuration, such as music and vocals, could work as well. These are known as *stems,* and using them is the common way of mixing for film.

Usually the dubbing mixers (the mixers who control the final dialogue, music, and effects mix of a film) much prefer stems from the music mixer rather than the full mix, so they have more control over the music mix when they add the dialogue and sound effects. The way the stems are usually broken out is:

- The drums and percussion

- Bass

- The rest of the music

- The lead instrument or vocals

- Any instruments with a lot of high frequencies, such as triangle, bells, or piccolo

By using the same idea and mixing in stems, you can compress each stem individually and have a lot more control as needed (see Figure 5.2). Of course, it will take more time and computer horsepower as well, as your mix grows in sophistication.

Setting the Compressor

In most modern music, compressors are used to make the sound "punchy" and in your face. The trick to getting the punch out of a compressor is to let the attacks through and play with the release to elongate the sound. Fast attack times will reduce the punchiness of a signal, while slow release times will make the compressor pump out of time with the music.

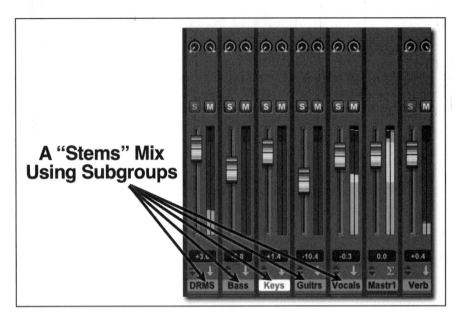

Figure 5.2 Stem mixing.

Because the timing of the attack and release is so important, here are a few steps to help set it up. Assuming you have some kind of constant meter in the song, you can use the snare drum to set up the attack and release parameters. This method will work the same for individual instruments as well.

1. Start with the slowest attack and fastest release settings on the compressor.

2. Turn the attack faster until the instrument (snare) begins to dull. Stop at that point.

3. Adjust the release time so that after the snare hit, the volume is back to 90 to 100 percent of normal by the next snare beat.

4. Add the rest of the mix back in and listen. Make any slight adjustments to the attack and release times as needed.

The idea is to make the compressor "breathe" in time with the song.

Typical Buss Compressor Settings

The buss compressor is typically set at a very low compression ratio of 1.5 or 2 to 1, with only a dB or two of compression, but the gain is then increased until the song's overall volume level is comparable to the hits of the genre of music you're working in (see Table 5.1).

If you use a brickwall limiter for a client mix, set it so that the level never exceeds 0.1 dB, so there will be no digital overs. You can further tweak the amount of compression by increasing the output of the compressor or the input of the limiter.

Table 5.1 Typical Buss Compressor Settings

Parameter	Setting
Ratio	1:1.5 or 1:2
Attack	50 ms or slower
Release	Auto if available, 250 ms or faster
Gain Reduction	Inserted toward the end—1 or 2 dB
	Inserted at the beginning—3 or 4 dB

In the case of buss compressors, not all are up to the task. Some impart too much of their own sound into the mix, while others may be way too slow to be of much use. Because usually only 2 or 3 dB of compression may be all that's added (although it can be a lot more under the right circumstances), the compressor itself actually adds an intangible sonic quality. That being said, T-RackS has a couple of modules that work very well for buss compression.

Classic Compressor Typical Settings

With T-RackS standard, we're in luck because the Classic Compressor fits the bill perfectly. Because its attack time is so slow, it's pretty difficult to cut any of the transient attacks from the drums; plus the Sidechain HPF is perfect for keeping the bottom end under control. Table 5.2 shows typical settings, which are a good reference point to start from.

Table 5.2 Classic Compressor Mix Buss Settings

Parameter	Setting
Sidechain HPF	70 Hz—increase or decrease to control the bottom of the mix
Attack	20 ms
Release	100 ms—increase or decrease to breath with the track
Ratio	3:1
Input Drive	0 dB—increase for more compression
Output	0 dB—increase for more level

Vintage 670 Typical Settings

One of the all-time favorites of mix engineers everywhere is the Fairchild 670, which is a part of T-RackS Deluxe. Back in the bad old hardware days, it was pretty rare to see one in a studio, because they were expensive ($25,000), were hot and heavy, and required a lot of maintenance to keep them working. Thankfully, you can have virtually the same sound from within T-RackS. Table 5.3 provides some settings to get you started.

Table 5.3 Vintage Tube Compressor (Fairchild 670) Mix Buss Settings

Parameter	Setting
Time Constant (Left and Right)	5 or 6 depending upon the type of music
Input (Left and Right)	Increase until meters read 2 to 3 dB of gain reduction
Threshold	3—increase to make the compression more aggressive-sounding
AGC	Link
Output	0 dB—increase for more level

Brickwall Limiter Typical Settings

As you raise the output level of your buss compressor, you'll find that the transient peaks will cause the Overload indicators to light. To stop that from happening and to get a nice, loud mix for your client, it's best to have the buss compressor feed into the Brickwall Limiter to keep the peaks under control. Table 5.4 contains some typical settings.

Table 5.4 Typical Mix Buss Settings for the Brickwall Limiter

Parameter	Setting
Input	0 dB—increase for more level (and to make the mix louder)
Attack	6 ms—increase or decrease for transient control
Release	30 ms—increase or decrease to breath with the track
Output Ceiling	0.1 dB
Style	Clean for transparent peak limiting

Summary Questions

You can find answers to the Summary Questions in the Appendix at the end of this book.

1. Why did the use of buss compression begin?

2. What is a client mix?

3. What are the advantages of inserting a mix buss compressor toward the end of your mix?

4. What are the advantages of inserting a mix buss compressor at the beginning of your mix?

5. What are the disadvantages of inserting a mix buss compressor at the beginning of your mix?

6. What is an alternative to buss compression?

7. What is a stems mix?

8. What's the best way to set up a buss compressor to get a punchy track?

9. What happens if the attack time is set too fast on a buss compressor?

10. What happens if the release time is set too fast on a buss compressor?

6 Preparation for Mastering

Although many new mixers think that the process is just push up the faders, balance the mix, add some EQ, adjust the pans, add some effects, and you're finished, that's actually not how it works. There are a number of additional items to keep in mind during a mix besides the mixing process itself. Many less experienced engineers may not be aware of these issues in the first place, and some mixers that are aware sometimes forget in the heat of audio battle.

What am I referring to? Let's take a look at the concerns beyond making your mix sound tall, deep, and wide.

How Long Should It Take to Complete a Mix?

Many musicians and engineers who haven't worked on a record-label project have nothing to compare their experiences to, so they're not always sure when a mix is finished. How long should a mix take, anyway? When you first start out, you fly through mixes and think you're finished after an hour or two, but then you begin to discover that there's a lot more to it than you ever conceived. As always, the only way that you can gauge what you're doing is by comparing yourself to a pro.

Let's assume for a second that you decide you're going to have someone else mix your songs, either because a record label is demanding it or because you just think it's a good idea to employ someone with skills better than yours so you can watch and learn. (You should be applauded if you think this way.)

In the days of analog consoles, we used to figure that a mix would take anywhere from a day to a day and a half per song, especially if you used an A-list mixing engineer. The first day was used to get the mix 95 percent of the way, and the second half-day was to eke out as much of that extra 5 percent as you could with a fresh set of ears. Although you might get lucky on the first mix that took a day and a half, it was not uncommon to continue remixing from there until everyone was happy, which for a big-budget legacy act could take six or eight weeks on the same song. For example, legendary engineer Bruce Swedien states that there were 91 mixes of Michael Jackson's "Billie Jean," and they wound up choosing number 2. And it took U2 six full weeks to find the perfect mix for "I Still Haven't Found What I'm Looking For." Don't let that amount of time alarm you; there were more songs mixed in the day-and-a-half timeframe (or less) than there ever were in six weeks.

Of course, the time it takes for a mix depends upon the song, the type of material, how it was recorded, the number of tracks and elements, and the mixer himself. If the recording was a live concert with a power trio and a vocalist, for instance, and all the songs sounded pretty much the same in quality, and there were no huge fixes required (which is a rarity), an entire album might only take a day to finish. On the other hand, an R&B song that was 100 tracks wide could take the mixer a few days just to get a handle on what's actually there and what's actually needed in the mix. And a song that had poorly recorded tracks that needed a lot of editing and fixing to bring it up to snuff might take even longer than that. On the other hand, producer/engineer Kevin Shirley has been known to mix entire albums in a single day, such as the best-selling Journey records he worked on in the '80s—but that's because he actually started his mix early in the project, from his very first rough mix.

Regardless of how long the initial mix took in the analog days, tweaks or changes after the fact were once dreaded by all involved because resetting the console and all the outboard gear almost always resulted in a mix that sounded slightly different (not to mention the time of setting things up again—see Figure 6.1). As a result, producers and mixers did everything they could to avoid any redos, which mostly consisted of taking

Figure 6.1 The reason why no one with a console wants to remix.

extra time on the mix to be sure that it sounded as perfect as possible, mixing multiple versions of the song (more on this in a bit), and doing just about anything to ensure that they had a final version of the song in some way, shape, or form when they walked out that studio door at the end of the day. Now, with mixing "in the box" in a DAW, it's easy to recall a mix exactly to where you left it days, weeks, months, or even years before, making mix fixes fast and easy as long as you're not using any outboard gear and you have the same plug-ins installed. As a result, this has taken some of the pressure out of the mixing process, unless you're still mixing in the analog world with a console and outboard gear. Then mixing hasn't really changed much at all.

When Is a Mix Finished?

So when is a mix considered finished? Here are some guidelines:

1. **The groove of the song is solid.** The groove usually comes from the rhythm section, but it might come from an element like a rhythm guitar (such as on the Police's "Every Breath You Take") or just the bass by itself, such as anything from the Detroit Motown that James Jamerson played on (Marvin Gaye's "What's Goin' On" or the Four Tops' "Reach Out (I'll Be There)" and "Bernadette," for instance). Whatever element supplies the groove, it has to be emphasized so that the listener can feel it.

2. **You can distinctly hear every instrument.** Every instrument must be in its own frequency range in order to be heard clearly. Depending upon the arrangement, this is what usually takes the most time during mixing.

3. **Every lyric and every note of every line or solo can be heard.** You don't want a single note or word to be buried. It all has to be crystal clear. Use your automation. That's what it was made for.

4. **The mix has punch.** The relationship between the bass and drums must be in the right proportion for them to work together well so the song has a solid foundation.

5. **The mix has a focal point.** What's the most important element of the song? Make sure it's obvious to the listener.

6. **The mix has contrast.** If you have the same amount of the same effect on everything (a trait that's heard in many of the mixes by beginner engineers), the mix will sound washed out. You have to have contrast between different elements, from dry to wet, to give the mix depth.

7. **All noises and glitches are eliminated.** This means any count-offs, singer's breaths that seem out of place or too loud because of vocal compression, amp noise on guitar tracks before and after the guitar is playing, bad-sounding edits, and anything else that might take the listener's attention away from the track.

8. **You can play your mix against songs that you love, and it holds up.** This is perhaps the ultimate test. If you can get your mix in the same sonic ballpark as many of your favorites (either things you've mixed or things from other artists) after you've achieved the previous seven items, then you're probably home free.

In the end, it's best to figure at least a full day per song regardless of whether you're mixing in the box or on an analog console, although it's still best to figure a day and a half per mix if you're mixing in a studio with an analog-style console. Of course, if you're mixing every session as you go along during the recording process, then you might be finished before you know it, because your mix might be in such terrific shape that all you need are just a few tweaks.

Mixing in the Box

Whereas once upon a time it was assumed that any mix was centered around a mixing console, that's not entirely true anymore. Because DAWs have become so central to everyday recording, a new way of mixing has arrived—mixing in the computer without the help of a console, or mixing "in the box."

Many old-school mixers who grew up using consoles disliked mixing in the box because they found it hard to mix with a mouse, and they didn't like the sound. Although it's true that the sound of the very early workstations didn't sound as good as what everyone was used to at the time, that's no longer the case today. Indeed, even the analog-to-digital converters in the least expensive DAW interfaces have come a very long way, so the sound of them is not the issue that it once was. Another objection has been that the sound of the internal mix buss of a DAW degraded the signal, and once again that isn't quite the case anymore. It's true that each DAW application uses a different algorithm for summing the instruments in the mix buss, which makes the sound vary from a little to a lot, but a bigger issue is the same one that has faced mixers in the analog world almost from the beginning—it's how you drive it that counts!

What has changed with in-the-box mixing is the way that you can mix multiple songs at the same time. No longer are we restricted to working on a single song like in the days of analog. Now it's possible to work on several songs all at the same time. (In fact, I know a lot of big-name mixers who work this way.) It's great if you suffer from ADD, but I think it actually helps to work on several songs at once because the project (assuming it's more than a single song) takes on a more cohesive sound. In the analog days, when a mix was built around a console, it was common to have some songs that sounded really different from others on the same album after they were mixed. The songs might have used the same players, been recorded in the same studio, and been mixed on the same console with the same outboard gear, but there were always a few songs that just sounded different. Now when you work on multiple mixes at once, the sound of each of them tends to get a bit closer to one another, since you can make an instant comparison to what sounds good and what sounds deficient with every mix.

Suffice it to say that whether you're mixing in the box or with a traditional console, the principles are the same. Although you may have a preference for one or the other, you can expect similar quality from either mixing method.

Alternative Mixes

It's now standard operating procedure to do multiple mixes in order to avoid having to redo the mix again at a later time because an element was mixed too loudly or softly. Even with the ease of calling up a digital project in a DAW, a mixer does not want to revisit a project when it's complete if at all possible. To avoid a remix, the mixer will do alternate mixes that take into account any element that might be questioned later (such as lead vocal, solo instrument, background vocals, and any other major part) and will provide a separate mix with that particular track recorded slightly louder and again slightly softer. These are referred to as the *up mix* and the *down mix*. Usually these increments are very small: 1/2 dB to 1 dB, but usually not much more. (Yes, that small of an increment does make a difference in a tight-sounding mix.)

There are all sorts of ways that alternate mixes can be valuable at a later time. Here's how:

- It's easy to correct an otherwise perfect mix later by simply pasting in a masked word from one of your alternate mixes.

- It's easy to substitute a chorus with another that might have softer background vocals (for instance) without going back to remix.

- An even more common occurrence is when an instrumental mix is used to splice out objectionable language during mastering.

Although many record companies ask for more or different versions, here's a typical version list for a mix from a rock artist. Other types of music will have a similar version list that's appropriate for the genre.

1. Album Version

2. Album Version with Vocals Up

3. Contemporary Hits Radio Mix—Softer Guitars

4. Album-Oriented Radio Mix—More Guitars and More Drums

5. Adult Contemporary Mix—Minimum Guitars, Maximum Keyboards and Orchestration

6. TV Mix (the entire mix minus lead vocal)

The artist, producer, or A&R person may also ask for additional versions, such as a pass without delays on the vocals in the chorus, more guitars in the vamp, or a version with bass up. There is also a good chance that any singles will need a shortened radio edit as well if you're working with a hit artist who's on the radio (something that happens less and less these days).

Thanks to the virtues of the digital audio workstation and modern console automation, many engineers leave the up and down mixes to an assistant, since most of the hard work is already complete.

The TV Mix

Although mixing in the box has made alternative mixes so easy to make that some are being eliminated until requested, the one alternative mix that will always have a place is the TV or instruments-only mix. This is a mix with everything but the lead vocal (and sometimes background vocals, too), so the artist or band can appear on television and appear to be playing live. This is useful because not many television shows have the time for sound check and the audio resources to allow a band to play live, so the TV mix is a convenient compromise.

Another use for the TV mix is for use as background music for television shows, movies, or commercials. Although it may not be used for these purposes if a song is a hit, it has become a nice source of additional income for artists and bands. As a result, a TV mix is almost always done along with the final master mix of a song.

Mixing with Mastering in Mind

Regardless of whether you master your final mixes yourself or take them to a mastering engineer, things will go a lot faster if you prepare for mastering ahead of time. Nothing is as exasperating to all involved as not knowing which mix is the correct one or for-getting the file name. Here are some tips to get you "mastering ready."

- **Don't over-EQ when mixing.** It's better to be a bit dull during mixing and let your mastering engineer brighten things up. In general, mastering engineers can do a better job for you if your mix is on the dull side rather than too bright or too big.

- **Don't over-compress when mixing.** You might as well not even master if you've squashed it too much already. Hyper-compression (see Chapter 10) deprives the mastering engineer of one of his major abilities to help your project. Squash it for your friends. Squash it for your clients. But leave some dynamics for your mastering engineer. In general, it's best to compress and control levels on an individual-track basis and not that much on the stereo buss except to prevent digital overs.

- **Having the levels match between songs is not important.** Just make your mixes sound great; matching levels between songs is one of the reasons you master your mixes.

- **Getting hot mix levels is not important.** You still have plenty of headroom even if you print your mix with peaks reaching –10 dB or so. Leave it to the mastering engineer to get those hot levels. It's another reason why you do it.

- **Watch your fades.** If you trim the heads and tails of your track too tightly, you might discover that you've trimmed a reverb trail or an essential attack or breath. Leave a little room and perfect it in mastering, where you will probably hear things better.

- **Document everything.** You'll make it easier on yourself and your mastering person if everything is well documented, and you'll save yourself some money too. The documentation expected includes any flaws, digital errors, distortion, bad edits, fades, shipping instructions, and record company identification numbers. If your songs reside on hard disk as files, *make sure that each file is properly IDed for easy identification* (especially if you're not going to be at the mastering session).

- **Alternate mixes can be your friend.** A vocal up, vocal down, or instrument-only mix can be a lifesaver when mastering. Things that aren't apparent while mixing sometimes jump right out during mastering, and having an alternative mix around can sometimes provide a quick fix and keep you from having to remix. Make sure you document them properly, though.

- **Check your phase when mixing.** It can be a real shock when you get to the mastering studio, the engineer begins to check for mono compatibility, and the lead singer or guitar disappears from the mix because something in the track is out of phase. Even though this was more of a problem in the days of vinyl and AM radio, it's still an important point because many so-called stereo sources (such as television) are either pseudo-stereo or only stereo some of the time. Check it and fix it before you get there.

Summary Questions

You can find answers to the Summary Questions in the Appendix at the end of this book.

1.   What is mixing in the box?

2.   What's the greatest advantage of mixing in the box?

3.   What's the average amount of time that a mixer likes when using a console?

4.   List five ways that you know your mix is finished.

5.   What is an up mix?

6.   List two ways that alternate mixes may come in handy.

7.   Give three examples of alternative mixes.

8.   What is a TV mix?

9.   Why is mono compatibility of the mix so important?

10.   Why are hot mix levels not important to give to mastering?

7 Introduction to Mastering

The term "mastering" is either completely misunderstood or shrouded in mystery, but the process is really pretty simple. Technically speaking, mastering is the intermediate step between mixing the audio and preparing it to be replicated or distributed. But it's really much more than that.

Mastering is the process of turning a collection of songs into a record by making them sound like they belong together in tone, volume, and timing (spacing between songs).

That's the whole key to mastering—taking a collection of songs and making them sound like they belong together. The collection can be of songs you've recorded that will be released together, such as an album, or it can be of songs by other artists, such as a compilation album. Regardless, you want all your songs to sound at least as good as what you're used to listening to.

All too often people have the misconception that mastering is only about EQing the track to make it sound bigger, but it's really the process of making a collection of songs sound similar enough that they can be played back to back and sound the same in tone and volume, as well as be played back to back with the "hits" and still hold up.

Here's when you need mastering:

- If you have a song that sounds pretty good by itself but sounds quiet when played after another song, you need to master it.

- If you have a song that sounds pretty good by itself but sounds too bright or dull next to another, you need to master it.

- If you have a song that sounds pretty good by itself but sounds too bottom heavy or bottom light against another, you need to master it.

Here's what mastering is not: It's not a set of tools or a device that you run music through and it automatically comes out mastered. It's more of an art form that mostly relies on an individual's skill, experience with various genres of music, and good taste.

Mastering is a simple process, but like all simple processes, it's a lot more involved than it seems when you really get into it. As long as you know a few tricks and don't have beyond-reality expectations for the end result, it can improve your program material by varying degrees, or it can just as easily make it a lot worse than what you started with.

Just like everything else in music and recording, it's now possible to master your own material, and T-RackS 3 is an excellent tool to do it with. As you've seen, T-RackS works well as a plug-in with your DAW, but it's also a great stand-alone mastering application. T-RackS 3 now makes mastering very inexpensive compared to previous audio generations, but just because you own a hammer doesn't mean that you know how to swing it.

Before we get into the mechanics of mastering, let's take a look at what this process called "mastering" really is.

Why Master Anyway?

Mastering should be considered the final step in the creative process, since this is the last chance to polish and fix a project. A project that has been mastered simply sounds better if done well. (That's the key phrase, of course.) It sounds complete, polished, and finished. The project that might have sounded like a demo before now sounds like a "record." Here's why:

- The mastering engineer has added judicious amounts of EQ and compression to make the project bigger, fatter, richer, and louder.

- He's matched the levels of each song so they all have the same apparent level.

- He's fixed the fades so that they're smooth.

- He's edited out distorted parts or glitches so well that you didn't even notice.

- He's made all the songs blend together into a cohesive unit.

- In the case of mastering for CD or vinyl, he's inserted the spreads (the time between each song) so the songs flow seamlessly together.

- He's sequenced the songs so they fall in the correct order.

- He's also made and stored a backup clone in case anything should happen to your cherished master.

- He's taken care of all of the shipping to the desired replication facility if you're using one.

And all this happened so quickly and smoothly that you hardly knew it was happening.

The Difference between You and a Pro

If we really break it down, a mastering pro usually has three things over what you do at home.

- **The gear.** A real pro mastering house has many things available that you probably won't find in a simple home or small studio DAW room, such as high-end A/D and D/A converters, a great-sounding listening environment, and an exceptional monitoring system.

  The monitoring system of these facilities sometimes costs far more than many entire home studios. Cost isn't the point here, but quality is, since you can rarely hear what you need to hear in order to make the adjustments that you need to make on the near-field monitors that most recording studios use. The vast majority of monitors and the rooms in which they reside are just not precise enough.

- **The ears.** The mastering engineer is the real key to the process. This is all he does day in and day out. He has "big ears" because he masters at least eight hours every day and knows his monitors the way you know your favorite pair of sneakers. Plus, his reference point of what constitutes a good-sounding mix is finely honed, thanks to working hours and hours on the best- and worst-sounding mixes of each genre of music.

- **A backup.** I don't know who said it, but this phrase rings true: "The difference between a pro and an amateur is that a pro always has a backup." It's good advice for any part of recording, but especially for mastering. You wouldn't believe the number of times masters get lost. This is the one thing that you can do just as well as a pro can, with no trouble at all!

But I'm betting that you don't have the money to use a pro, and you have this great piece of software in T-RackS, so here's how you can master your songs yourself.

The Mastering Technique

Here's what you're trying to accomplish by mastering:

- Raise the level of the songs so that they're competitive with others on the market

- Make them all sound the same in relative level and tonal quality

- Finish them by editing out count-offs and glitches, fixing fades, adding PQ and ISRC codes, and creating spreads for CDs and vinyl records

- Export them as MP3, AIFF, or WAV files

Before we can learn more about these items, we have to set up T-RackS first.

Setting Up T-RackS 3 for Mastering

T-RackS 3 is unique because of its stand-alone mode that allows you to do just about every mastering function that you need in a single package. The T-RackS 3 stand-alone can be broken down into seven sections. They are:

1. **The presets.** This area is used to save and load T-RackS presets. These presets can be saved or loaded as a global preset (for the entire mastering chain) or by module (for each of the processor modules).

2. **The signal chain.** In this section, the modules are loaded into the 12 available slots. The first four slots can be configured in parallel for sophisticated signal processing chains when necessary.

3. **The processor interface.** This section is where the controls of each selected process are manipulated.

4. **Metering section.** This is an extensive section containing all the meters required for mastering. This section is always visible.

5. **Comparison settings.** The A-B-C-D buttons allow you to store different signal chain settings in each for quick comparisons.

6. **Preferences panel.** This section consists of four buttons for authorization, version information, preferences, and automation settings.

7. **File Editor.** This section shows a waveform of the topmost file and allows basic editing features, such as fades, snapshots, and loop points.

Figure 7.1 shows the different sections

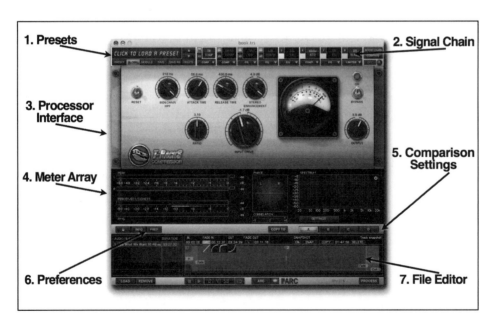

Figure 7.1   T-RackS 3 stand-alone sections.

Setting Up the Project Parameters

When you launch the stand-alone version of T-RackS 3, an untitled project is loaded by default. It has the following properties (see Figure 7.2).

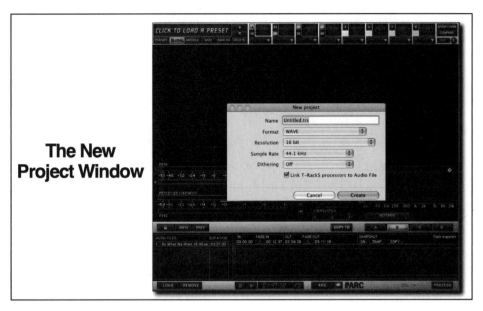

The New Project Window

Figure 7.2   New project window.

- Output file format: WAV

- Output sampling rate: 44.1 kHz

- Output resolution: 16-bit

- Dithering: Off

Although this setting might work on many projects that you're working on (especially if the final product is intended for CD delivery), it's best to know what your options are. Let's take a look at each. It's important to remember that the settings chosen here will be the final settings for your project exports after you've finished mastering.

The Export Format
T-RackS allows you to choose between four different file formats for your exports:

- WAV

- AIFF

- CAF

- SDII

There's really no difference between AIFF and WAV files these days. Once upon a time, you'd use an AIFF audio file if you were on a Mac and a WAV file if you were on a PC, but both platforms now happily read either one without any difficulty.

SDII files are a different story, though. This is a file format that Digidesign introduced during the early days for their Sound Designer II application, which was the precursor to the now widely used Pro Tools. Although the format has the advantage of storing a limited amount of metadata, its use has diminished over the years, and it's not entirely compatible with all playback software and DAWs. The only time SDIIs are completely safe to use is if your export is expressly intended for Pro Tools, but even then I'd stay with a WAV or AIFF file format in case you ever decide to use another DAW in the future.

T-RackS 3 also exports to the new Core Audio Format, which is designated by a .CAF filename extension. This format was developed by Apple around its Core Audio technology for use with operating systems 10.4 and higher, and it is designed to overcome some of the limitations of the older WAV and AIFF file containers.

A CAF file doesn't have the 4-GB limit of the other formats, and it can theoretically hold a file that is hundreds of years long. (That's a big file!) The format is also able to hold practically any type of audio data and metadata, any number of audio channels, and auxiliary information, such as text annotations, markers, channel layouts, and other DAW data. One of the more interesting features of CAF as a file container is that you can append new audio data on the end of the file, making it ideal as an archive format.

All Apple software products, including GarageBand and QuickTime Player, now support CAF files and can open them directly. If you want CAF files to be played on other systems, convert them to WAV or MP3 files with a utility such as Factory Audio Converter.

File Resolution

If your final export is intended for CD, online, and video, then 16-bit is what you want. If the highest quality audio is required for DVD or Blu-ray disc, then 24-bit is the correct setting. Even though 32-bit, 32-bit float, and 64-bit float potentially provide much higher quality, chances are that you've not recorded in the other resolutions, so consider them there for a future delivery application.

The resolution options are:

- 16-bit
- 24-bit
- 32-bit
- 32-bit float
- 64-bit float

Never go higher than the resolution that your project started at, however, because you gain nothing in quality, and your file will be a lot larger. For instance, if your project started at 16-bit, selecting 24-bit or higher buys you nothing.

Sample Rate

The sample rate is similar to the resolution parameter in that there are a couple of selections that are commonly used, and the others are available if ultra-high quality is desired. The majority of the time, 44.1 kHz and 48 kHz will be used—44.1 if exporting for CD or an online service, and 48 kHz if the final destination is film, television, DVD, or Blu-ray disc. The other resolutions can now be distributed by Blu-ray, but just like with resolution, if your project started at 48 kHz (your mix files), you gain nothing by exporting to a higher sample rate, and your file will need a lot more storage space as a result.

The sample rate options are:

■ 44.1 kHz

■ 48 kHz

■ 88.2 kHz

■ 96 kHz

■ 176.4 kHz

■ 192 kHz

Dithering

Dither is a low-level noise signal that is added to the program in order to trim a large digital word into a smaller one. Because a CD and most online services require that the word length must be 16 bits, a program with a longer word length (like the usual 24 bits as used in a DAW) must eventually be decreased. Just lopping off the last 8 bits degrades the audio (called *truncation*), so the dither signal is used to gently accomplish this task. Since word lengths usually expand when a signal undergoes digital signal processing (up to as many as 64 bits), eventually it must be reduced to 16 bits to fit on a CD or for MP3 or AAC encoding. An undithered master will have decay trails stop abruptly or will have a buzzing type of distortion at the end of a fadeout.

The dithering options are:

■ Off

■ On

There are two rules for dither that must be observed; otherwise, it won't have the desired effect.

■ **Dither the signal once and only once.** Because dither is a noise signal, it will have a cumulative effect if applied more than once. Plus, dither introduced too early in the signal chain can have a very detrimental effect on any subsequent digital processing operations that occur afterward.

■ **Dither only at the end of the signal chain.** T-RackS 3 does this automatically.

Link to Audio File

The final selection links the T-RackS processor settings to each audio file that you import. If you leave this unselected, all of your imported files will have the same processor settings. This is not something you want if you're mastering music and each song is different, in which case you'll want to check this selection. If you have a project that could use the same settings for every import, such as pieces of a podcast or dialogue editing for film, then leave the option unchecked.

Loading Files

You can load files into T-RackS 3 in two ways—by simply dragging and dropping them into the Audio Files panel or by using the Load button to select them from a menu (see Figure 7.3). The audio files then appear in the Audio Files panel with their durations next to them (see Figure 7.4), and the waveform of the top file appears in the Waveform panel. You can change the sequence of files by simply dragging and dropping within the panel.

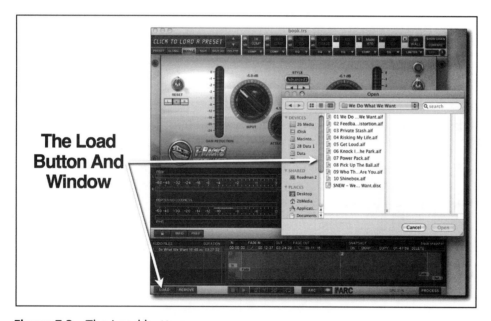

Figure 7.3   The Load button.

To play the file, click the green Play button (see Figure 7.4) or hit the spacebar on your computer keyboard. Hit the Stop button or the spacebar again to stop playing. You can skip to any spot within the song by placing your cursor at that spot on the waveform (see Figure 7.4).

The Preferences

You can access the Preferences window by selecting the Pref button. This window contains some useful settings (see Figure 7.5).

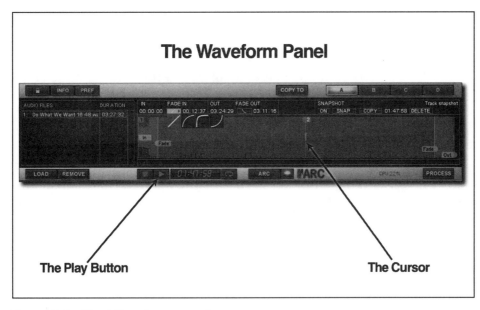

Figure 7.4   The Waveform panel.

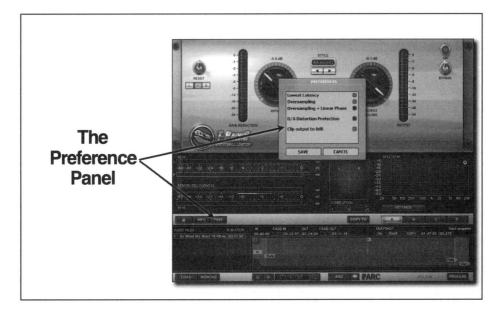

Figure 7.5   The Preferences window.

- **Lowest Latency.** Latency isn't usually a factor when T-RackS is in stand-alone mode, but if you're using it to process a mix in real time, then you need the lowest latency possible. This selection lowers the latency to just 132 samples. Under most circumstances, however, you should keep this preference deselected.

- **Oversampling.** Many plug-ins raise the sample rate in order to more precisely perform the digital processing, which is called *oversampling*. This results in a cleaner sound. Keep this selected *unless* the following preference is selected.

■ **Oversampling + Linear Phase.** This is an extension of the Oversampling preference and allows the Linear Phase mode of the Linear Phase Equalizer to perform, thereby increasing the smoothness of the equalizer. Selecting this preference raises the total latency to 19,684 samples, but that shouldn't be a problem for mastering situations. Keep this selected.

■ **D/A Distortion Protection.** When you have a file with an extremely hot level, there's a chance that a phenomenon called *intersample distortion* will occur. These are peaks that occur between the samples that may go into overload but aren't picked up by the level meter or overload indicator. Even though the playback doesn't sound distorted while playing back in T-RackS, distortion may occur during playback on inexpensive playback units, such as MP3 and CD players with less sophisticated D/A and analog electronics. By selecting this preference, the Brickwall Limiter will keep this under control *as long as it's the last processor in the signal chain*. Keep it selected.

■ **Clip Output to 0 dB.** This option limits the signal to 0 dB by hard-clipping the signal. If you set up your mastering signal chain correctly, this preference doesn't need to be selected. Keep it deselected.

Summary Questions

You can find answers to the Summary Questions in the Appendix at the end of this book.

1. What is mastering?

2. List two examples of when you need mastering.

3. List two differences between a pro and an amateur.

4. What are you trying to accomplish by mastering?

5. What is an SDII file?

6. What is a CAF file?

7. What are three advantages of the CAF format?

8. What file resolution is required for CD, online, and video?

9. What is gained by exporting a file at a higher resolution than you started with?

10. What is the sample rate for film and television?

8 Monitoring during Mastering

The single greatest impediments to doing your own mastering are your monitoring system and monitoring environment. It doesn't matter whether you're mastering in your bedroom or in a million-dollar SSL room with George Augspurger acoustics (he's considered the father of modern studio acoustic design), you're at a huge disadvantage if you master on the same monitors that you mixed on. Why? Because all monitors have flaws, and if you use the same monitors for mastering, you're either overlooking the problem or just compounding it to make it even worse.

Let's say that your monitors have a bit of a dip at 2 kHz (which is not uncommon, since that's the cross-over point of most near-field monitors). While recording and mixing, you boost 2k to compensate for what you're not hearing. Now, it might sound okay on these monitors during mastering, but if you play it back on another set of speakers, you might find that the midrange is tearing your head off.

Now let's bring the environment into the equation, which compounds the problem. Let's say that between the monitors you're listening to (say a typical two-way system with a 6- or 8-inch woofer) and your room, you're not hearing anything below 60 Hz or so. To compensate, you add +8 dB of 60 Hz so it sounds the way you think it should sound. If you master on the same monitors in the same environment, you'll never know that when you get the song outside of your studio, it will be a big, booming mess.

I know, you can't afford Vincent van Haaff (another well-regarded studio acoustician) to trick out your garage, and those Ocean Way monitors are still about $40,000 out of reach. Don't worry, there's still hope.

Monitoring Techniques for Mastering

Regardless of what kind of monitors or room you have to work with, there are some proven techniques that will yield some reasonable results even under the worst conditions. These all depend upon your ears, which are still the primary ingredient in mastering, and not the gear.

1. **Listen to some CDs that you love first.** You want to listen to the highest quality program that you can get, so this is one time when the CD beats an MP3 (although a FLAC file could work). Listen to a favorite record or two that you know really well and you understand how it sounds on a variety of systems,

and then try to match it. This one point will save you from over- or under-EQing. If your mastering job doesn't sound similar to your reference record, then you're not finished yet. It doesn't have to sound exactly like it, but it has to sound in the ballpark. If the bottom end is thumping on your reference and your mastering is not, then you have to try something else (or have the song remixed). If, on the other hand, your bottom is big and full and your reference song is not, then you can be sure that you're going to have way too much bottom when you play the song on a system in the outside world. If you do nothing else, this one trick will help you more than anything else.

2. **Establish two different listening levels.** You need one level that you would consider fairly loud, where you can easily hear how the lower-frequency instruments (especially bass and drums) sit with each other, and another that's at a much lower listening level, somewhere near the point where you can hold a conversation while the music is playing. Use these two listening levels only. Mark them down on your volume control, make a note where the level is in the software, and do whatever you have to do to make these two levels repeatable. The levels are somewhat arbitrary in that they depend on your monitors and your environment, but the idea is that you want one level that's loud enough for you to gauge the low end and another that's quiet enough that you can hear the tonal balance. If you listen at varying levels, your reference point will be thrown off, and you'll never be sure exactly what you're listening to, which is why you keep it to two levels only.

3. **Use two sets of speakers—a large set and a small set.** Even if the largest speaker system that you can afford is a two-way bookshelf speaker with a 6-inch woofer, you should have an even smaller set to reference against. Although not the best, even a pair of computer speakers will do as long as you can feed them from the same source as your large set. The only way that you can ever be sure how things really sound is if you have two different sets to reference against. Mastering pros usually use a huge set of monitors with double 15-inch woofers plus a subwoofer, and an average two-way bookshelf speaker or even smaller. Even if you have more than two sets of monitors available, limit your listening choices during mastering so you don't confuse yourself and end up chasing your tail.

Summary Questions

You can find answers to the Summary Questions in the Appendix at the end of this book.

1. What are the greatest impediments to doing your own mastering?

2. Why is mastering on the same monitors you mixed on not a good idea?

3.   What's the most important thing to do before you begin to master?

4.   Why should you limit your listening to only two different levels?

5.   Why is a second set of monitors necessary for mastering?

6.   What is the primary ingredient in mastering?

7.   How do you prevent yourself from over- or under-EQing?

9 Metering

etering is extremely important in mastering—much more so than mixing—especially when you're trying to achieve hot levels. But there are more metering tools available to the mastering engineer than the simple metering that we're used to during recording, because the mastering process requires a lot more visual input to tell you the things that you need to know.

Typically, the mastering engineer will look at the following:

- A PPM meter (Peak Program meter)

- An RMS meter

- A spectrum analyzer (sometimes called a *real-time analyzer* or *RTA*)

- A phase correlation meter

- A phase oscilloscope

Fortunately, T-RackS 3 includes all these meters plus one more—a Loudness meter that features optimal zones for different styles and genres of music. Let's take a look at them.

The Peak Meter

The Peak meter was created by the BBC when they realized that the common VU meter (see Figure 9.1) wasn't precisely telling an engineer exactly what the program signal was doing, which is especially important in broadcast, where over-modulation of the signal can bring on the wrath of the government. The standard VU (which stands for *Volume Units*) meter, which was common on all professional audio gear until the late '90s, only shows the average level of a signal and has a very slow response time, so you'd have to guess at the signal peaks, since they were too fast for the meter to read them. A good example of this effect takes place during recording of a high-pitched percussion instrument, such as a triangle or tambourine, where the signal is almost all peaks, so the knowledgeable engineer would record the instrument at a barely visible −20 on the VU meter to keep the recording from distorting. Couple the slow response of the VU meter with the fact that it was an analog mechanical device that could easily be knocked out of calibration, and you can see the need for a new metering system.

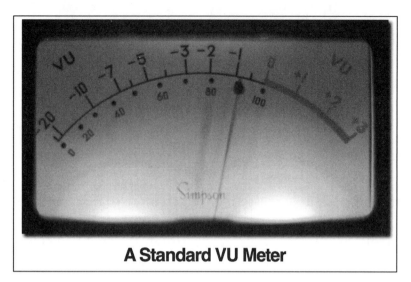

Figure 9.1 A VU meter.

The peak meter, on the other hand, has an extremely fast response, which is almost fast enough to catch most peaks (more on this in a bit) and can now be simulated on a digital display (such as T-RackS 3) instead of using an actual meter. (A hardware meter used to be very expensive before the digital age.) The peak meter also became a necessity for digital recording because any signal beyond 0 dB causes a very nasty distortion. As a result, all peak meters now have a red Over indicator that lets you know you're exceeding the zone of an audibly clean level.

In T-RackS 3, the Peak meter provides a precise, sample-accurate indication of the instantaneous peak level, complete with a Peak-Hold function. (How long it holds the peak can be adjusted in the Preferences.) The ever-present red Over indicators light only when there are more than three consecutive 0-dB samples, which is a situation you want to avoid at all costs by using a module such as the Brickwall Limiter and adjusting the Ceiling value so it never goes beyond −0.1 dB.

A not too well-known phenomena is called *inter-sample distortion,* where the signal peaks exceed 0 dB between the samples (and are never indicated by the Overload indicator as a result) on really hot signals. This can cause trouble when the song or program is played back later on a CD or MP3 player and the digital-to-analog convertor (D/A) is overloaded, even though the Overload indicator never lights (which is why some mastered programs sound so harsh). T-RackS 3 compensates for this with a selection in the Preferences called *D/A Distortion Protection,* which allows the Brickwall Limiter to keep it under control as long as the unit is placed in the last position of the processing chain.

The Peak meter also has three scales that can be selected by clicking on the Settings button and selecting the Peak Meter section (see Figure 9.2). All three are useful, depending upon the situation.

Figure 9.2 Peak meter settings.

- **−90 .. 0 dB.** This is a general-purpose scale that displays everything from a very low-level (−90 dB) signal to a peak of 0 dB.

- **−50 .. +5 dB.** This scale looks at the signal from between −50 to +5 dB. It's used primarily to look at signals that go beyond 0 dB.

- **−60 .. 0 dB.** This scale zooms into the portion of the scale around 0 dB so you can precisely see how much headroom is still available.

The RMS Meter

The RMS meter is a digital version of an old VU meter discussed a little while back. RMS stands for the *root mean square* measurement of the voltage of the electronic signal, which roughly means the average. In T-RackS 3, the RMS meter combines both left and right channels into a single display that measures the power of a signal. Even when your Peak meter is tickling 0 dB, the RMS meter will be settled at a point a lot lower, since it is much slower reacting and is measuring the signal differently than the Peak meter.

The frequency response of the RMS meter is flat, which can give you a false sense of level if the song has a lot of low end. For that reason, it's best to read the meter in conjunction with the other meters to give you an idea of where you're at in terms of level and loudness. (They're different, as you'll soon read.) One thing that the RMS meter is very good at is telling you whether two (or more) songs are approximately the same level. Don't rely on the meter, though—you have to use your ears to make the final determination.

The Perceived Loudness Meter

The Perceived Loudness meter is not normally found in the mastering chain, but it's often seen in broadcasting. It determines how "loud" a program is by measuring all the frequencies that make up the program and then applying a weighting measurement to the frequency bands in proportion to how the ear perceives them. For example, the ear is most sensitive in the 2- to 4-kHz range, so frequencies at 100 Hz or 10 kHz can measure 15 dB higher in level than a 4-kHz tone, yet they'll seem equally loud.

As I said before, level and loudness are two different things. In the case of mastering, level consists of the signal voltages that you read on a meter, and loudness is what you hear.

Two different programs can have identical peak and RMS levels, yet one can still sound louder than the other. A great example is the difference in loudness between a television program and the commercials around it. They're both at exactly the same level (most stations are very strict that a peak never goes beyond −10 dB), but the commercials seem much louder than the program. The Perceived Loudness meter attempts to provide a more reliable indication of the loudness by frequency weighting of the program.

The key to the Perceived Loudness meter is the Loudness Suggestions in the Settings menu. Select the genre of music that you're mastering, and you will see a green and red line at the bottom of the meter. The green area indicates where most loud passages should peak, while the red area indicates where most loud passages peak during extreme conditions or on very loud masters. The Suggested areas were determined by averaging a number of commercial productions in the particular genre, so they're a pretty good comparison for the genre.

The Phase Scope

The Phase "Scope" gets its name from the fact that in the early days of recording, the phase between the left and right channels was checked by using an old-fashioned oscilloscope (see Figure 9.3), which was nicknamed a "scope." Phase is extremely important in a stereo signal, because if the left and right channels are not in phase, not only will the program sound odd, but instruments panned to the center (such as lead vocals and solos) may disappear if the stereo signal should ever be combined into mono.

Although you may think that mono isn't used much these days, you'd be surprised. If your song is ever played on AM radio, it's in mono on 99 percent of the stations. On FM radio, if a station is far away from where you're listening, the stereo signal may collapse into mono because the signal strength is weak. On television, it's not uncommon for the stereo to be automatically converted to mono depending upon the network. Sometimes the settings in the iTunes player can be switched to mono, or a stereo song can be ripped in mono, so they'll play back in mono on an iPod or MP3 player. Mono is everywhere, so it's a good thing to pay attention to the phase of your program.

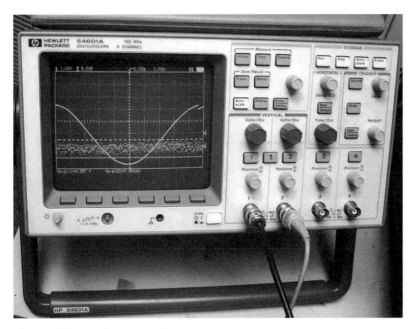

Figure 9.3   A classic oscilloscope.

The Phase Scope isn't very good for measuring absolute levels (that's why you have the other meters), but it does provide a wealth of information about stereo source positioning and the relative phase and level between the two channels. The signals are displayed in a two-dimensional pattern along the X and Y axes called a *Lissajous figure* (see Figure 9.4). An identical signal on both channels results in a 180-degree vertical line representing a central, mono signal (see Figure 9.5), while a true stereo signal will give you a more or less random figure that's always moving (see Figure 9.6).

Figure 9.4   A Lissajous figure on an oscilloscope.

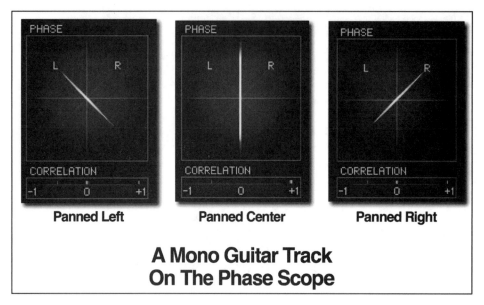

Figure 9.5   A mono signal on the Phase Scope.

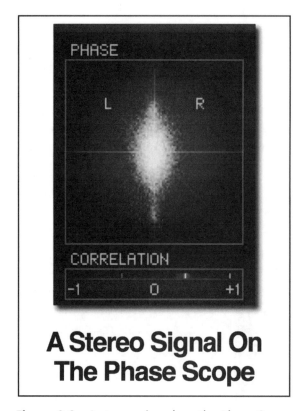

Figure 9.6   A stereo signal on the Phase Scope.

After you watch the Phase Scope for a while, you'll see that you can instantly tell a lot about the signal as you recognize the different shapes it can take on with different signals. For instance, a vertical line that goes straight up and down means that the signal is in perfect mono (refer to Figure 9.5), while a vertical line that lays flat across means that the signal is perfectly out of phase, and anything at 45 degrees is fully panned. Go beyond 45 degrees, and your sound starts to go out of phase. Simpler and nearer sounds, such as mono one-shots or notes and chords, are illustrated by thick, bold-looking solid lines. Widen the stereo image, and you'll see a relatively wider and stringier image. Heavily reverberated or delayed sounds form shapeless images with lots of small dots. The complex arrangements normally found on most records will show all these and everything in between. The more defined the borders are, the more of the signal is above 0 dB. As you can see, the Phase meter shows everything from the width, phase, panning, amplitude, and even clipping info in the signal.

The Phase Scope in T-RackS 3 has a number of different parameters that can be selected from the Settings panel. You can set the Scope to display the samples with dots or lines and select various display speeds. A Normalize function makes the Scope display the signal at the same width regardless of the level, which works well for very low-level signals.

The Phase Correlation Meter

While the Phase Scope takes some time to get the hang of, the Phase Correlation meter is dead simple. Anything drawn toward the right-hand "+1" side of the meter is in phase, and anything drawn toward the left-hand "−1" side of the meter is out of phase.

In general, any meter readings above 0 and in the right-hand, positive side of the scale have acceptable mono compatibility. A brief readout toward the left-hand negative side of the scale isn't necessarily a problem, but if the meter consistently sits in the negative side, it could represent a mono compatibility issue. Keep in mind that the wider your stereo mix is, either by panning or wide stereo reverbs, the more the Phase Correlation meter will tend to indicate toward the left side; but as long as the signal stays mostly on the right, your compatibility should be good to go.

Verify the Phase Issue

If the Phase Correlation meter or Phase Scope indicates that there might be a mono compatibility problem, it's important to immediately listen in mono to verify whether it's an issue and whether the track is acceptable. In the event that the out-of-phase condition is verified, sometimes flipping the phase of one channel can fix it, but usually a remix may be the only answer.

What to Do with Out-of-Phase Material

A track can be out of phase for a number of reasons.

- **Acoustic phase.** A mic is too close to another and picks up the same source, such as on a drum kit. This occurs often during a tracking session with a lot of instruments playing at the same time, where the results may present a mono compatibility issue.

■ **Electronic phase.** This occurs when the polarity of a mic cable is reversed (Pins 3 and 2 are accidentally reversed), the phase switch on a console or mixer is accidentally or mistakenly engaged, or some other cable in a studio is mis-wired. (It happens even in the biggest of studios.) If this occurs when you're recording a multi-miked drum kit, it can never be undone. If it happens on a guitar or bass, you can flip the phase back during mixing.

Most of the time, if a severe mono compatibility problem is found during mastering, there's little that the mastering engineer can do except to send the track back to be remixed. There's an outside chance that using the M/S function on the T-RackS 3 compressor modules just might control the phase enough to make the mono compatibility acceptable.

The Spectrum Analyzer

The Spectrum Analyzer is an excellent tool for determining the frequency balance of your program by looking at it in sixth-octave portions. It's especially effective for singling out particular frequencies that are too hot and for dialing in the low end.

The Spectrum Analyzer has a number of parameters that can be adjusted from the Settings menu.

■ **Scales.** Just like with the Peak meter, the Spectrum Analyzer has the ability to choose between two scales.

> **−90 .. 0 dB.** This provides a vertical scale that shows signals as low as −90 dB (which is pretty quiet).

> **−60 .. 0 dB.** This sets the lowest part of the scale at −60 dB, effectively zooming in by only looking at the top 60 dB of the scale.

■ **Curve or Bars.** This selects whether the frequency curve is drawn with yellow bars or with sixth-octave segments. This is strictly an engineer's choice. Some feel they can see the bars better, while others prefer the segments.

■ **Tilt value from 0 to 9 dB.** The Tilt value compensates for the natural high-frequency roll-off that occurs in almost all program material. The 0-dB value has a flat frequency response with white noise (which doesn't represent music very well). Basically, the higher the value of Tilt, the more even the higher frequencies will look on the Analyzer even though they're rolled off. It's a way of helping you gauge whether any of the high frequencies are louder or softer than the others as the Tilt is increased.

■ **Response Type.** There are three types of responses that can be selected, each with its own particular use.

> **Peak.** This works just like the Peak meter, with the signal peaks instantly responding to the frequency peaks of the material in a particular frequency

band. How fast the Analyzer responds is adjusted with the three selections at the bottom of the menu: 250ms (very fast), 500ms (medium fast), and 1000ms (slow). Peak is the setting to use when you need an instant picture to see whether there are any frequency areas that might be giving you trouble.

RMS. This sets the Analyzer to react like the RMS meter, which shows you more of the power of the song, because the response is slower and less sensitive to the peaks of the program.

Average. This is the slowest of the three selections, as it takes an average of 30 seconds of program to determine an easy-to-read display of the overall frequency balance. Keep in mind that it will reset if the music is stopped, and it will take 30 seconds to average everything again. You can also reset the Average display by clicking on the Analyzer.

■ **Channel Display.** This parameter allows you to select whether the Analyzer reads the left and right program combined (L+R), only the left channel (L), or only the right (R). L+R is the usual selection.

■ **Analyzer Resolution.** This is the number of sampling points per sixth-octave segment. The higher values (8k and 16k) give you a more accurate picture and are particularly effective for observing the low frequencies below 100 Hz.

■ **Show Peaks.** This enables the peak hold function of the Analyzer, which is useful when the Peak Response is chosen and the Analyzer's response is very fast.

How to Use the Spectrum Analyzer

Contrary to what you might think, when you look at the Analyzer, the object is not to aim for a totally flat response. The deep bass (below 40 Hz) and the ultra-highs (above 10k) are almost always rolled off compared to the other frequencies (see Figure 9.7). It's very useful to look at songs, CDs, mixes, or any program that you think sounds really good and get a feel for what it looks like on the Analyzer. Keep in mind that your mastering job will probably not look like your chosen example, since each song is unique, but if it's in the same genre, it might be close by the time you've finished working your mastering magic.

1. Make sure that no frequency is a lot hotter (such as 4 or 5 dB) than the others. Use one of the EQ modules to tame that particular frequency band.

2. Unless the Tilt is selected, make sure that there's a gentle roll-off above 10 kHz. The roll-off is natural and occurs in every type of program.

3. Make sure there's no excessive energy below 40 Hz, especially if your speakers don't reproduce these frequencies. Too much energy in this area usually just makes everything sound muddy and ultimately doesn't add anything to the program.

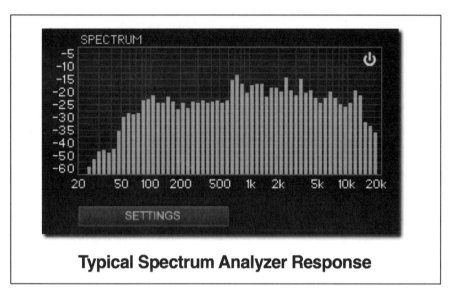

Figure 9.7   A typical response on the Spectrum Analyzer.

Typical Settings

There are obviously a lot of parameter settings in the Meter section of T-RackS 3, so here's a set that you can start from. Keep in mind that each song and genre of music is unique, so what works for one song may not work for others.

Meter Parameter	Setting
Peak meter	−60 .. 0 dB
Peak Loudness meter	Choose your style of music
Spectrum Analyzer	Bars
Scale	−60 .. 0 dB
Tilt value	6 dB
Response Type	Peak
Channel Display	L+R
Analyzer Resolution	8k
Show Peaks	Enabled

Summary Questions

You can find answers to the Summary Questions in the Appendix at the end of this book.

1.   What's the difference between a peak meter and a VU meter?

2.   What does VU stand for?

3. What's the best way to avoid lighting the red Over indicators?

4. Why does the RMS meter always read a lot lower than the Peak meter?

5. Why do frequencies at 2 to 4 kHz seem louder than the rest of the spectrum?

6. What's the difference between level and loudness?

7. Why are commercials frequently louder than the television programs around them?

8. List three examples of where mono might be used.

9. What can happen if the channels of a song are seriously out of phase?

10. How can you tell whether something is out of phase by reading the Phase Scope?

10 Mastering 101 (The Mastering Process)

Now that you've seen the basic philosophy of mastering, let's tackle the creative aspects. By and large, you're trying to make the track sound better and similar to songs released by the major record labels, and the way to do that is by adjusting the audio level and audio EQ as needed. Let's look at audio level first.

Adjusting the Audio Level

Not all volume levels are created equal. How we perceive the volume level of a song and how we compare it to something else are two different animals. Not only that, if we try too hard to make a song loud, we can actually make it so unenjoyable to listen to that few people will listen more than once. So getting your audio level as loud as you can without destroying it may be the number-one job of mastering today.

Perceived Audio Level

The amount of perceived audio volume without distortion (on an audio file, CD, vinyl record, or any other audio delivery method yet to be created) is one of the things that top mastering engineers pride themselves on. Notice the qualifying words "without distortion," since that's the trick—to make the music as loud as possible (and thereby competitive with other products on the market) while still sounding natural. Be aware that this generally applies to modern pop/rock/R&B/urban genres and not as often to classical or jazz, whose listeners much prefer a wider dynamic range where maximum level is not a factor.

Competitive Level

The volume/level wars really began way back in the vinyl era of the '50s, when it was discovered that if a record played louder than the others on the radio, the listeners would perceive it to be "better" sounding and would make it easier to become a hit as a result. Since then, it's been the job of the mastering engineer to make any song intended for a distribution medium like radio as loud as possible in whatever way he can.

And of course, this also applies to situations other than the radio. Take the iPod, CD changer, or, in the very old days, record jukebox. Most artists, producers, and labels certainly don't want one of their releases to play softer than their competitors' because of the perception (which is not necessarily the truth) that it doesn't sound as good if it's not as loud.

But the limitation of how loud a "record" (we'll use this term generically) can actually sound is determined by the delivery medium to the consumer. In the days of vinyl records, if a mix was too loud, the stylus would vibrate so much that it could lift right out of the grooves and the record would skip, or an expensive cutting stylus ($15,000 in 1960s dollars) would burn out from too much level. When mixing too hot to analog tape, the sound would begin to softly distort, and the high frequencies would disappear (although many engineers and artists actually like this effect). When digital audio and CDs came along, any attempt to mix beyond 0 dB Full Scale would result in terrible distortion as a result of digital "overs." (Nobody likes this effect.)

So trying to squeeze every ounce of level out of the track is a lot harder than it seems, and that's where the art of mastering comes in.

Hyper-Compression: Don't Go There!

That being said, over the years it has become easier and easier to make a record that's hotter and hotter in perceived level, mostly because of new digital technology that has resulted in better and better limiters. Today's digital "look ahead" limiters make it easy to set a maximum level (usually at −0.1 or −0.2 dB FS) and never worry about digital overs and distortion again, but this can come at a great cost in audio quality if you're not careful.

Too much buss compression or over-limiting either when mixing or when mastering results in what has become known as *hyper-compression*. Hyper-compression is to be avoided at all costs because:

- It can't be undone later.

- It can suck the life out of a song, making it weaker-sounding instead of punchier.

- Lossy codecs such as MP3 have a hard time encoding hyper-compressed material and can insert unwanted side effects as a result.

- Studies have shown that it causes listener fatigue, so the consumer won't listen to your record as long or as many times.

- A hyper-compressed track can actually sound worse over the radio (if you care about airplay at all) because of the interaction with the broadcast processors at the station.

A hyper-compressed track has no dynamics, leaving it loud but lifeless and unexciting. On a DAW, it's a constant waveform that fills up the DAW region in the timeline. Here's how the levels have changed on recordings over the years, using this hit recording from the '80s and its subsequent reissues as an example (see Figure 10.1).

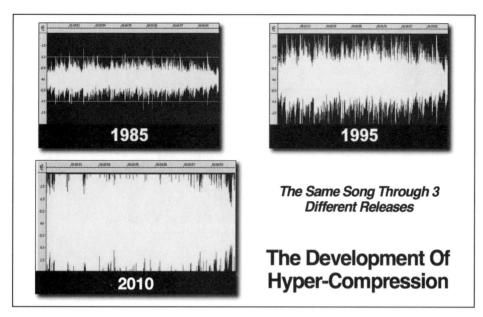

Figure 10.1   An example of hyper-compression.

But getting the most level onto the disc or file is not the only level adjustment that the mastering engineer must practice. Just as important is the fact that every song on the disc must be perceived to be just as loud as the next. Once again, "perceived" is the key word, because this is something that can't be directly measured and must be done by ear.

How to Get Hot Levels

The bulk of the audio level work today is done by a combination of two of the mastering engineer's primary tools: the compressor and the limiter, which you'll use as two plug-ins during mastering. The compressor is used to increase the small- and medium-level signals, while the limiter controls the instantaneous peaks. Remember, though, that the setup and sound of the compressor and limiter will have an effect on the final audio quality—maybe for the worse, especially if you push them too hard.

The Signal Chain

Although the equalizer might change position from before the compressor to after, the usual signal chain looks like what you see in Figure 10.2.

The limiter is *always* the last in the chain, no matter how many other devices you add and in which order, because that's what adds any additional level and stops any overs from happening.

The compressor will give you the apparent level and is equally as important as the limiter to the mastering process. If you want to master like the pros, you must use both.

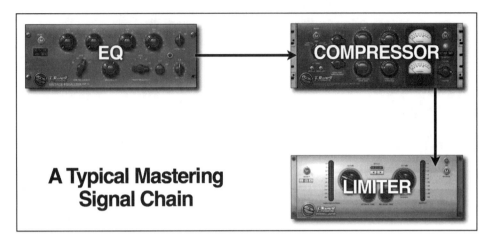

Figure 10.2   The typical mastering signal chain.

The Limiter

To understand how a limiter works in mastering, you have to understand the composition of a typical music program first. In general, the highest peak of the source program (the song, in this case) determines the maximum level that can be achieved in a digital signal. But because many of these upper peaks are of very short duration, they can usually be reduced in level by several dB with minimal audible side effects. By controlling these peaks, the entire level of the program can be raised several dB, resulting in a higher average signal level.

Most digital limiters used in mastering are *brickwall* limiters. This means that no matter what happens, the signal will not exceed a certain predetermined level, and there will be no digital overs. Thanks to the latest generation of digital limiters, louder levels are easier to achieve than ever before because of more efficient peak control. This is thanks to the look-ahead function that just about all digital limiters now employ. Look-ahead delays the signal a small amount (about 2 milliseconds or so) so that the limiter can anticipate the peaks in such a way that it catches them before they get by. Analog limiters don't work nearly as well because an analog input can't predict its input like a digital limiter with look-ahead can. Since there is no possibility of overshoot, the limiter then becomes known as a *brickwall* limiter.

By setting a digital limiter correctly, the mastering engineer can gain at least several dB of apparent level just by the simple fact that the peaks in the program are now controlled.

The Compressor

As the names imply, compression is primarily used to increase the lower-level signals, while a limiter is used to decrease the loud ones.

The keys to getting the most out of a compressor are the Attack and Release (sometimes called Recovery) controls, which have a tremendous overall effect on a mix and therefore are important to understand. Generally speaking, transient response and percussive sounds are affected by the Attack control setting. Release is the time it takes for the gain to return to normal (zero gain reduction).

In a typical pop-style mix, a fast Attack setting will react to the drums and reduce the overall gain. If the Release is set very fast, then the gain will return to normal quickly but can have an audible effect of reducing some of the overall program level and attack of the drums in the mix. As the Release is set faster, the gain changes that the drums cause might be heard as "pumping," which means that the level of the mix will increase and then decrease noticeably. Each time the dominant instrument starts or stops, it "pumps" the level of the mix up and down. Compressors that work best on a wide range of full program material generally have very smooth release curves and slow release times to minimize this pumping effect.

Rules for Hot Levels

Setting the levels may be the most important part of mastering, since it will determine not only the competitive and perceived level, but also whether all the songs being mastered sound like a cohesive collection. Here's how you do it:

1. Set the master level on the limiter to −0.1 or −0.2 dB to contain the peaks and avoid digital overs.

2. Set a compressor at a ratio of 1.5:1 or 2:1 to gain apparent level. Generally speaking, the trick with compression in mastering is to use either a slow release time or one that's timed to the drums and less (usually much less) than 5 dB of compression.

3. Adjust the attack time to let the desired amount of transients through. The slower the attack time, the punchier the sound (generally speaking).

4. Adjust the release time to avoid pumping. Time it to the track to keep it punchy-sounding. Set it to slow to keep it smooth-sounding.

5. Increase the level of the program to the desired level by increasing the Output control of the compressor.

6. Compare the song to other songs in the mastering session until they're all at the same level. (Use your ears, not the meters.)

Mastering Compressor Tips and Tricks

Adjusting the Attack and Release controls on the compressor and/or limiter can have a surprising effect on the program sound.

■   Slower Release settings will usually make the gain changes less audible but will also lower the perceived volume.

- A slow Attack setting will tend to ignore drums and other fast signals but will still react to the vocals and bass.

- A slow Attack setting might also allow a transient to overload the next piece of equipment in the chain.

- Gain changes on the compressor caused by the drum hits can pull down the level of the vocals and bass and cause overall volume changes in the program.

- Usually only the fastest Attack and Release settings can make the sound "pump."

- The more bouncy the Level meter, the more likely that the compression will be audible.

- Quiet passages that are too loud and noisy are usually a giveaway that you are seriously over-compressing.

Frequency Balance

EQing is usually the place that gets engineers mastering their own mixes into trouble. There's a tendency to overcompensate with the EQ, adding huge amounts (usually of bottom end) that wreck the frequency balance completely.

The first rule to avoid this is:

1. **Listen to other CDs (no MP3s) that you like first, before you touch an EQ parameter. The more CDs you listen to, the better.**

You need a reference point for comparison, or you'll surely overcompensate.

The second rule is:

2. **A little EQ goes a long way. If you feel that you need to add more than 2 or 3 dB, you're better off mixing the song again!**

Whereas in recording, you might use large amounts of EQ ($+/-3$ to 15 dB) at a certain frequency, mastering is almost always in very small increments (usually in tenths of a dB to 2 or 3 at the very most in rare cases). What you will see is a lot of small shots of EQ along the audio frequency band, but in very small amounts.

For example, you might see something like -1 at 30 Hz, $+0.5$ at 60 Hz, 0.2 at 120 Hz, -0.5 at 800 Hz, -0.7 at 2500, $+0.6$ at 8 kHz, and $+1$ at 12. Notice that there's a little happening at a lot of places.

Seriously, though, if you have to add a lot of EQ, go back and remix. That's what the pros do. It's not uncommon at all for a pro mastering engineer to call up a mixer and tell him where he's off and suggest that he do it again.

The third rule is equally important.

3. **Keep comparing the EQed version to the original version as well as other songs that you're mastering.**

The idea of mastering, first of all, is to make the song or program sound better with EQ, not worse. Don't fall into the trap where you think it sounds better just because it sounds louder. The only way to understand what you're listening to is to have the levels pretty much the same between the EQed and pre-EQed tracks. That's why T-RackS is so great for mastering. It has an A/B function that allows you to compensate for the increased levels so that you can really tell whether you're making it sound better.

The fourth rule is:

4. **You have to keep comparing the song you're currently working on to all the other songs in the project that you've worked on.**

The idea is to get them all to sound the same. It's pretty common for mixes to sound different from song to song, even if they're done by the same mixer with the same gear, but it's your job to make the listener think that the songs were all done on the same day in the same way. They have to sound as close as possible to each other as you can get them—or at least reasonably close so they don't stand out.

As you can see, mastering isn't that difficult as long as you keep in mind exactly what you're trying to do, which is to make a group of songs sound like they belong with each other.

Remember: Even if you can't get the songs to sound just like your best-sounding CD, your mastering job will still be considered "pro" if you can get all the songs to sound the same in tone and volume!

Summary Questions

You can find answers to the Summary Questions in the Appendix at the end of this book.

1. What is competitive level?

2. What is hyper-compression?

3. Why should hyper-compression be avoided at all costs?

4. What is the normal maximum level setting of the limiter during mastering?

5. What is the typical mastering signal chain?

6. Which position in the signal chain will the limiter always be in?

7. Why is a compressor used in the mastering signal chain?

8.   What is the look-ahead function of a digital brickwall limiter?

9.   What types of sounds are most affected by the Attack Time control on a compressor or limiter?

10.   What is pumping?

11 Mastering with T-RackS 3

We've covered all the theory and principles, so now it's time to get down to actual mastering with T-RackS 3. The T-RackS 3 stand-alone mode is very powerful and, as a result, provides multiple variations on how to accomplish the same job. Let's take a look at some typical possibilities.

The Mastering Signal Chain

As I've pointed out in other chapters, the order of the signal chain for mastering is critical to accomplish all that's needed in modern music. The following sections provide some examples of how to accomplish the task.

A Simple Signal Chain

Figure 11.1 shows a typical mastering signal chain, with the Linear Phase EQ in the first position, the Vintage Compressor 670 in the second, and the Brickwall Limiter last.

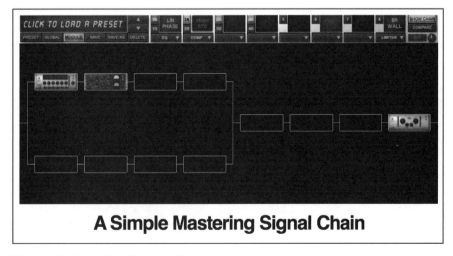

A Simple Mastering Signal Chain

Figure 11.1 A simple signal chain.

There are a couple of reasons for the EQ in the first spot. This is a leftover from the analog days when this processor order provided the best sonics when loading the program into a workstation from an analog source. In many cases, it simply wasn't possible to get enough gain from the output stage of the EQ without introducing some distortion (especially if one band was driven hard), while the compressor usually is designed for plenty of clean gain. That's not as much of an issue in the digital domain, especially if there are only small 2- and 3-dB increments of boost, but the EQ first in the chain still remains a popular order. The downside is that whatever frequency is being boosted by the EQ can be the first to trigger the compressor, which can give you some unexpected and unpleasant results. That's why it's okay to reverse the order of the processors, with the Vintage Compressor 670 in the number-one spot and the Linear Phase EQ in the second spot, especially if large increments of EQ need to be applied.

There is a general rule of thumb for compressor/EQ order that goes like this:

- If you're going to use a large amount of EQ, place the EQ after the compressor.

- If you're going to use a large amount of compression, place the compressor after the EQ.

The Brickwall Limiter will always be in the last position of the signal chain, especially if you want to take advantage of one of the preferences selected in Chapter 7—D/A Distortion Protection, where the Brickwall Limiter protects against inter-sample distortion.

Let's look at some typical processor settings.

The Linear Phase EQ

The Linear Phase EQ (see Figure 11.2) is used when you want nice, clean, uncolored equalization because the track already has the sound you're looking for.

Figure 11.2   The Linear Phase EQ.

The Linear Phase EQ is unique in a couple of ways. First, it has six bands of EQ, which is more than you'll usually see on an EQ, and it has a Linear Phase mode, which is entered by selecting the Linear Phase button on the bottom right (see Figure 11.3). The Linear Phase mode will change the sound of the EQ when selected, as it uses some extra computer horsepower to better align the phase of the filters and provide a bit more headroom, but this only works if you've selected Oversampling + Linear Phase in the

Preferences, as we discussed in Chapter 7. Try the switch in both positions and select the one that sounds best.

I like to use the LPEQ for adding a little "air" at 12 kHz, since it sounds so clean. It also works great with the low-frequency band engaged as a high-pass filter, passing all the frequencies above a certain frequency (see Figure 11.4). Sometimes a mix can clean up significantly by just rolling everything below 20 or 30 Hz.

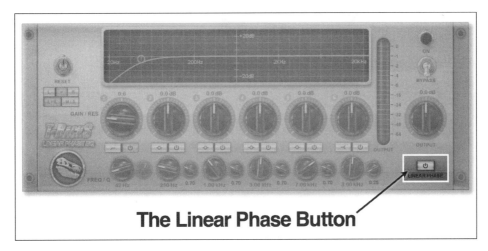

The Linear Phase Button

Figure 11.3   The Linear Phase button.

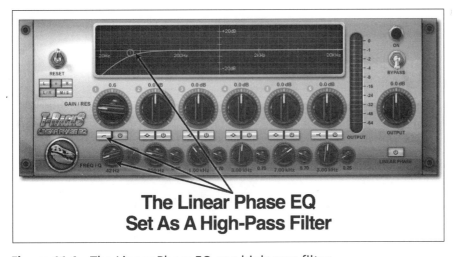

**The Linear Phase EQ
Set As A High-Pass Filter**

Figure 11.4   The Linear Phase EQ as a high-pass filter.

Yet another trick that's common to many of the processors in T-RackS 3 is the M/S mode, which is entered by selecting the button on the top left of the processor (see Figure 11.5). The M/S mode uses a Mid-Side matrix that allows you to select where the process works in the stereo image. The M assigns the process to the center of the stereo image as usual, but the S (or side) makes it seem as if the equalization is occurring at the outside edges of the stereo spectrum. Most of the time, you'll find that the Mid mode works best, but occasionally the Side mode will allow you to add EQ in a way that works better, such as brightening up a track without affecting a lead vocal.

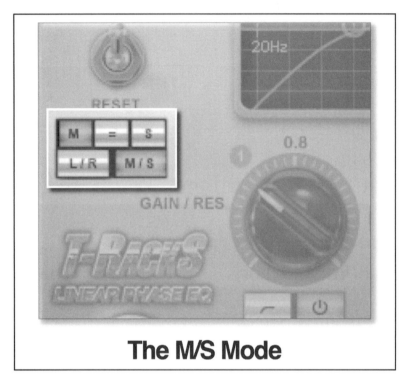

Figure 11.5   The M/S mode.

The Vintage Compressor Model 670

The Vintage Compressor 670 has long been a favorite of analog mastering engineers because of its smooth sound. It has a number of unique features that differ from most compressors (see Figure 11.6). First of all, the Threshold controls determine how hard or soft the compression knee will be. All the way to the left equals soft, and all the way to the right equals hard.

Second, the variable Time Constant control sets the compressor's attack and release times. Positions 1 through 4 are fixed from fast to slow, and positions 5 and 6 have dual time constants that work well on stereo programs.

Although it's not uncommon for gain reduction of 10 or even 20 dB to occur during tracking, it's a different story during mastering. You'll find that most pros use only a dB or 2 on most programs, and certainly no more than 3 or 4 in special cases. Many compressors, especially the Vintage 670, have a sound that you can hear even if they're in the signal path with almost no gain reduction. In any event, too much gain reduction will put you on the road to hyper-compression, so be careful.

Figure 11.6   The Vintage Compressor Model 670.

The compressor is usually where your apparent level will come from, and if the 670 is in the second position of the signal chain, raise the Output control to about 7 and then check the Gain Reduction meter on the Brickwall Limiter (not the Vintage 670). If the Gain Reduction meter is just flickering, you've got the gain about right. If not, raise the gain until it just barely lights. If it's consistently more than 2 or 3 dB of gain reduction, then decrease the output level of the Vintage 670.

Typical Vintage Compressor Model 670 Mastering Settings

Parameter	Setting
Time Constant	Position 1, 5, or 6
Threshold	About 2
Input Gain	1 to 3 dB gain reduction
Output	Increase to just below where the limiter (next in the signal chain) indicates gain reduction (between 7 and 9)

The Brickwall Limiter

The most critical component in the mastering signal chain is the Brickwall Limiter (see Figure 11.7), because it's the main line of defense for stopping overloads. The way this is done is by setting the Output Ceiling level to 0.1 dB.

Although you can certainly get a lot of program gain from the limiter, the louder it gets, the more compressed it sounds. This may be just the sound you're looking for, but most of the time you're in the ballpark if the input level meter is showing a few dB on the Gain Reduction meter on peaks.

The Attack and Release controls have more influence on the sound than almost any other parameter. The settings will be determined by the type of music, but in general, the punchier the sound, the longer the attack time and the shorter the release time.

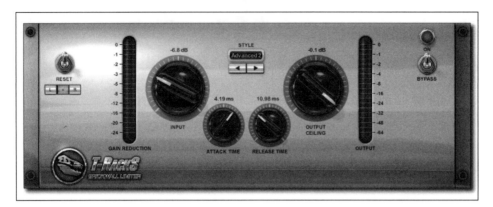

Figure 11.7 The Brickwall Limiter.

Although it may be tempting to turn each control to the max, that probably won't do you much good. If the attack time is too long, the limiter won't catch a lot of the peaks, and your track won't be as loud. If the release time is too short, you might hear the limiter working, which is something known as *pumping* or *breathing*. This is another reason why you can't set the controls the same for all the songs in an album. They're all different, and they all require unique settings to make them sound best.

An unusual feature of the Brickwall Limiter is the Style control, which can influence the overall sound of the song quite a bit. The Clean selection is indeed free of coloration, but sometimes that's not what you want, in which case Advanced 1, 2, 3, or 4 adds varying degrees of saturation mixed with the clean sound. If you really want your sound colored, then choose Sat 1, 2, or 3, which introduces full saturation. Note that the Gain Reduction meter doesn't work in these modes. The final mode is Clipping, which makes sure that the signal does not go beyond 0 dB, but it introduces some distortion as a result. Unless you like what it does to your sound, this mode should never be necessary if you set your signal chain properly.

Typical Mastering Settings for the Brickwall Limiter

Parameter	Setting
Output Ceiling	0.1 or 0.2 dB
Input	Adjust until peaks indicate a couple of dB of gain reduction
Attack	Start at 5 ms
Release	Start at 10 ms
Style	Start at Clean

Presets

A number of presets for different types of program material are available for each processor module. To load a preset, click on the Preset display (see Figure 11.8) and choose from the drop-down menu or click the up/down arrows and scroll through the available presets. The Preset button will open the Presets folder, letting you manually move, group, rename, and back up your preset files via a standard operating system window.

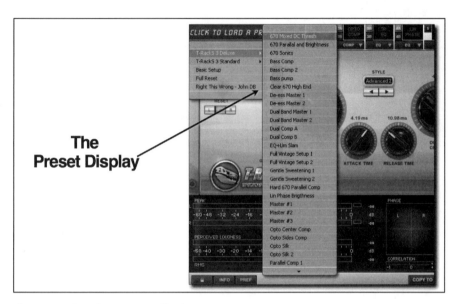

Figure 11.8   The Preset display.

If you come across a setting that you feel is particularly effective, you can save it as a preset. This applies to an entire T-RackS configuration or just a single module. The Save button saves the current T-RackS settings as a preset. Saving a preset with no previously loaded presets brings up the Save window (see Figure 11.9), where you are requested to select a save folder location on your hard disk (by default, this is the Presets folder) and give your preset a name. An Overwrite without Asking check box allows you to overwrite presets without being asked to confirm.

If you click on the Save button preset when you already have a preset loaded, a dialog box will prompt you to confirm that you want to save the settings over the currently loaded preset, unless you have checked Overwrite without Asking in the Save window.

The Save As button works like the Save button, presenting the Save window with the name of the current preset displayed in the preset name field and at the same time providing the option to save the preset to another one with a different name.

Delete Preset will delete the currently loaded preset, while the Global and Module buttons will allow you to save entire T-RackS settings or settings related to only the currently selected processor.

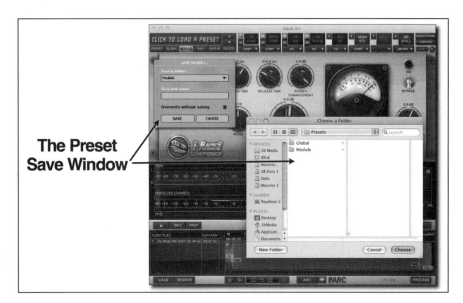

Figure 11.9   The Save window.

An Advanced Signal Chain

Many times the simple setup outlined here isn't sufficient for what your application requires. Almost any time that you feel you have to use a processor to an extreme (such as 10 dB of EQ or 6 dB of gain reduction), you're probably better off using a little bit of multiple processors instead to keep the signal clean, smooth, and punchy.

The EQP-1A Equalizer

Here's a signal chain where we'll add the Tube Program Equalizer EQP-1A for a bit of upper mids to get some snare drum snap and the Classic T-RackS Compressor to help the bottom end and widen the stereo image. These are in addition to the three modules we used in the first example. The signal chain would look like what you see in Figure 11.10.

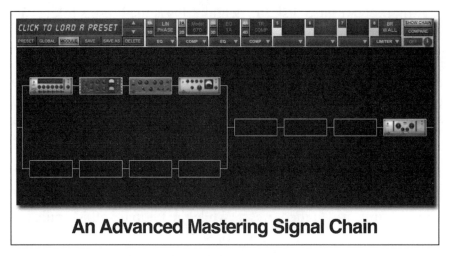

Figure 11.10   An advanced signal chain.

The EQP-1 is a totally unique equalizer, and as said before, nothing really sounds like it (see Figure 11.11). To bring out the snare snap, we'll set the High Frequency selector to either 3 or 4 kHz and slowly boost the High Frequency Boost control until we reach the desired effect. To add some nice bottom to the track, set the Low Frequency selector to 30 or 60 Hz and slowly increase the Low Frequency Boost control. You'll find that it's warm and round without sounding too big. For a nice sparkly top end, add a little 10 or 12 kHz.

Figure 11.11   The EQP-1 Tube Program Equalizer.

The EQP-1 is interesting in that it has both a Boost and an Attenuation control, but they're not at the same frequency so they don't cancel out. Sometimes you can more easily get the sound you're looking for by using both the Boost and Atten controls at the same time.

As with all T-RackS processor modules, don't be afraid to try the M/S function. It can really sound great sometimes.

The Classic Tube Compressor

The Classic Tube Compressor has a couple of neat features that work great for mastering (see Figure 11.12). The first is a sidechain high-pass filter, which allows the compressor to work on just the frequencies above what's selected by the control. In other words, if the Sidechain HPF control reads 100 Hz, that means that only the frequencies above 100 Hz will be acted on by the Classic Tube Compressor, and the frequencies below will not.

What this will effectively do is boost the low end, since it's not being compressed much. But be careful that the sound doesn't get too big. I think it's always best to put this processor early in a chain with another compressor following to keep the low end under control if you're going to use Sidechain HPF, but of course, it depends on the program and the engineer's taste.

Another interesting parameter that's unique to this processor is the Stereo Enhancement control, which affects the stereo imaging of the track. Turning it up will increase the

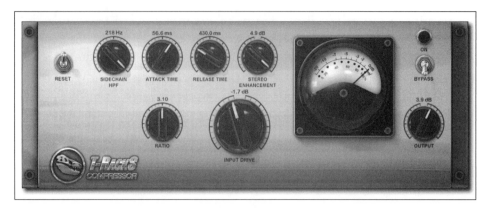

Figure 11.12   The Classic Tube Compressor.

stereo width, and turning it down (below 0 dB) will contract the stereo width. This works great if a track seems just a little too down the middle and it needs a little width. Keep your eye on the Phase Correlation meter as you add width to make sure that everything stays compatible.

As with any signal chain, make sure that your gain-staging is under control, meaning that the output level of a processor doesn't overload the next one in the chain. The last one in the chain before the Brickwall Limiter is the one to get the overall level boost from.

Parallel Processing

While it's possible to keep adding processors in the signal path, each doing a little bit instead of one processor doing a lot, remember that each processor is influenced by the previous one in the chain. Sometimes a better solution to the problem is parallel processing, and T-RackS 3 is perfectly configured for this with four additional parallel slots in the first four processor positions.

In this example, we're going to set our A chain up for some aggressive processing, while the B chain is set for smoothness. An Opto Compressor is added to the first position in the B chain and the EQP-1 in the second (see Figure 11.13).

The Opto Compressor

All optical compressors share a particular sonic character where the release time is rather gradual and is dependent upon the strength of the input signal (see Figure 11.14). The harder you hit it, the more gradual the release gets after the release time setting. This makes the Opto Compressor pretty smooth and a favorite on acoustic music. In this case we're going to set the ratio for about 2:1 with the typical slow attack and quick release. (It has a natural slow attack time anyway.) As with other compressor settings, we're going to set the Release control so the compressor breathes with the track. The Attack control setting sets how much of the highs get through and therefore determines how punchy the track will be.

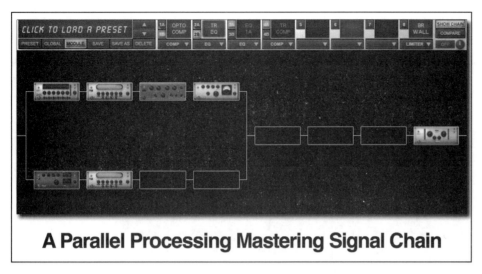

A Parallel Processing Mastering Signal Chain

Figure 11.13 A parallel processing example.

Figure 11.14 The Opto Compressor.

Like most hardware compressors, the Opto Compressor has the ability to monitor the input and output signal as well as gain reduction. The sound does change a little as soon as either the input or the output exceeds 6 dB or so, so be sure to monitor the level.

Typical Mastering Settings for the Opto Compressor

Parameter	Setting
Ratio	2:1
Compression	2.5 to 3
Attack	17 ms
Release	100 ms
Gain Reduction	2 to 4 dB

Show Chain

Sometimes it helps to see the chain graphically to understand exactly what kind of processing is occurring, especially in the case of parallel processing, where it's not readily apparent from just looking at the signal chain inserts. That's where the Show Chain button comes in (see Figure 11.15). Hit the button again to hide the graphic.

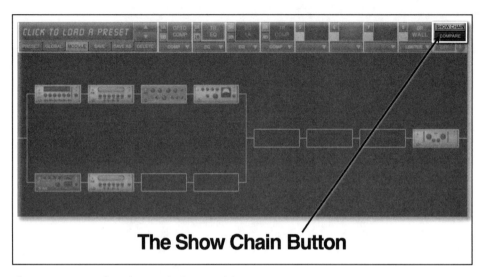

The Show Chain Button

Figure 11.15   The Show Chain graphic.

M/S Mastering

Using the M/S mode on many of the processors sometimes provides a benefit that can't be obtained with the usual L/R mode. High-energy middle signals (vocals, snare, bass guitars, and so on) can sometimes be easily separated from side signals (guitars, keyboards, cymbals, and so on). As a result, a processor in M/S mode can be used to process a single element instead of the whole mix. Even when things are sounding pretty good in L/R mode, it's always worth a quick check in M/S.

The Comparison Buttons

The A-B-C-D comparison buttons allow you to instantly switch between four completely different processor setups (see Figure 11.16). While it's possible to store totally different chains in each setting, it's most useful for comparison between individual processor settings. Let's say that you can't decide which sounds better: a 2-dB boost at 2 kHz or at 4 kHz. You can store one setting under the A button and the second under B and switch between them during playback to decide.

Another example would be if you're not sure of the difference between the time constant settings. By placing a setup under Button A using Time Constant 1 and another with Time Constant 5 under Button B, you can change back and forth while the track is playing to help you make your decision.

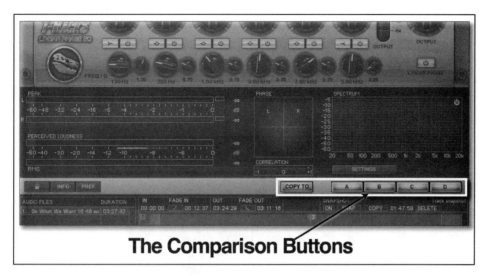

The Comparison Buttons

Figure 11.16   The comparison buttons.

And yet another example would be if you're just not sure of the difference in sound between having the equalizer in the first signal chain position before the compressor or after the compressor. Put the different settings on the comparison buttons and have a listen to help you decide which one works better.

To copy your settings, select the Copy To button. The four A, B, C, D buttons will start to flash. Click on any of them to save the settings under that button.

Remember that these settings are not stored in the session data, which is why it's best not to rely on this feature for different signal chain configurations.

The Compare Function

One of the most important functions on T-RackS 3 is the Compare function (see Figure 11.17). This lets you compare the original file to the one currently being processed. The key to this function is the volume knob that allows you to equalize the volume between the two. It's easy to think that the processed file is automatically better-sounding because it will be a lot louder, but it's only when both files are at the same level that you have a valid comparison.

The volume knob is not engaged until the Compare button is highlighted. Turn up the level until it equals the level when the Compare button is turned off. Be aware that without a limiter at the end of the Compare signal chain, the red Overload buttons will probably light. This won't hurt anything, although it might make the resulting sound a bit crunchy if the level is really hot.

By constantly comparing the sound while you're mastering, you can be sure that you're making the song sound better, not just different.

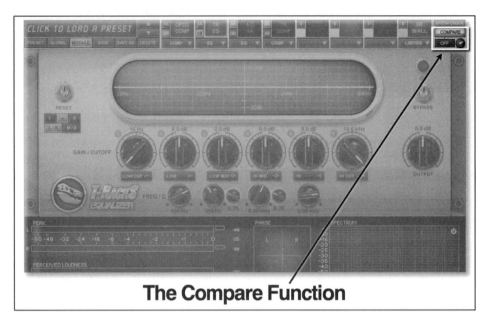

Figure 11.17   The Compare function.

The Waveform Display

T-RackS 3 also features a Waveform display that will show you the entire waveform of the audio file, but also will allow for finding a place within the song, setting loop points, trimming the audio file, and adding fades (see Figure 11.18).

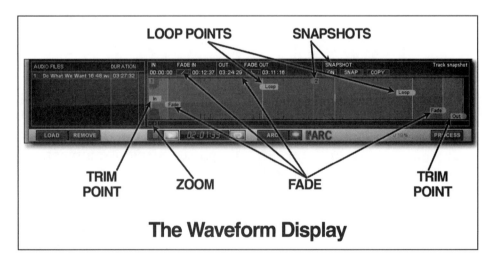

Figure 11.18   The Waveform display.

When Play is engaged, the yellow cursor moves across the waveform, and the counter shows the position. You can immediately go to any point of the song by clicking on that point of the waveform. You can also zoom in and out of the waveform by using the

+ and − buttons on the bottom left of the waveform display. (Look closely—they're tiny icons.) This comes in handy when you want to focus on a particular section of a song.

Trim

If you need to trim the beginning or end of a track, it's no problem with T-RackS. Simply move the green In or Out icons on the waveform, and the track begins and/or ends at that marker (refer to Figure 11.18).

Fades

Almost anyone with a workstation knows how to apply fades, but that doesn't necessarily mean that they're the right fades for the song. Another one of the main elements of a pro mastering job is making sure that the outro fade (if there is one) sounds smooth. As a result, you're frequently called upon to either apply the fade or help out one that's not quite the best it could be. T-RackS 3 has a Fade function that provides the necessary fade-ins and -outs as needed.

You can apply Fade In/Out to your file by positioning the green fade-in/out markers that appear at either end of the waveform (see Figure 11.18). By clicking on the In and Out markers, you set the In/Out points of your fade. The timing of the fade is set by moving the fade markers to the desired point in the song.

The fade-in or -out areas will be highlighted in green. The precise fade-in or -out time will be displayed over the waveform in the Fade panel. In this panel you can also select the type of fade required by clicking on the one of the curve icons.

Fade-Ins

There are two schools of thought on the fade-ins (sometimes called *headfades*). One calls for the use of a sharp "butt cut," and the other a more gradual algorithmic fade. Regardless of which type of fade is chosen, the principle is to get rid of count-offs, coughs, and noise left on the recording before the song begins. Although this seems to be an easy procedure, care must be used in order to maintain the naturalness of the downbeat. This is another task that should have been completed during mixing, but it's surprising just how much it's overlooked.

Fade-Outs

The type of fade selection used can make a big difference in the sound. The temptation is to use a linear curve to make a fade, but sometimes a logarithmic curve (see Figure 11.19) is smoother and much more realistic-sounding.

Even when a fade is made during the mix, it sometimes needs some help due to some inconsistencies, especially if it was done manually with a master fader. "Following the fade" means selecting a curve that approximates the one on the mix, only smoother.

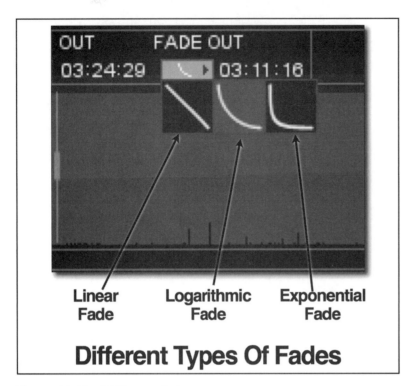

Figure 11.19   Different fade types.

Loops

If the Loop button is engaged, the song will automatically return to your start point after the song is played and will play again from there. Sometimes there's a section of the song that you need to loop in order to set some parameters, and these loop points can be set anywhere by simply dragging the loop point indicators to the desired points. Remember that the loop is only engaged if the green indicator on the transport panel is lit (refer to Figure 11.18).

Snapshots

Sometimes you need different processor parameter settings at different points in the song. This is made possible with a feature called *Snapshots*. To implement a Snapshot, simply change a parameter as needed and click on Snap on the Waveform display. A Snapshot (labeled Snapshot 2—Snapshot 1 is always at the beginning of the song) appears at the cursor point and can be moved to the exact position required by grabbing it with the mouse (refer to Figure 11.18). By clicking on the On button on the Snapshot panel, your parameter settings will change when the song reaches this point.

A Copy function is also included so you can make copies of snapshots. For instance, let's say that you want to change the EQ and compression when you reach the bridge of a song, but you want to return to the original settings as soon as the bridge ends. Simply copy Snapshot 1 and place the copy at the end of the bridge.

Summary Questions

You can find answers to the Summary Questions in the Appendix at the end of this book.

1. What is a disadvantage of putting an EQ before a compressor in the signal chain?

2. What's the rule of thumb for EQ/compressor order?

3. What is the maximum setting of the Output Ceiling control on the Brickwall Limiter before an overload occurs?

4. What controls have the most influence on the sound on the Brickwall Limiter?

5. What are the general settings of the Attack and Release controls on the Brickwall Limiter for a "punchy" sound?

6. Why can't you set your compressor and limiter the same for all the songs on an album?

7. What circumstances call for additional processors besides the main three normally used during mastering?

8. Why would you use M/S mode for mastering?

9. Why is the Compare function in T-RackS 3 so important?

10. Why would you apply a fade-in at the beginning of a song?

12 Exporting Your Project

The manner in which you export your songs or program is dictated by the distribution method for the export. Even though CDs are falling in popularity, they're still sold in the hundreds of millions and will be around for a while, so this chapter will take a look at what you need to know to meet your CD needs, as well as best encoding practices for online material. First, let's look at the export process in T-RackS.

Exporting in T-RackS 3

After you're satisfied with your mastering, exporting is easy. Simply select the Process button (see Figure 12.1). You'll be asked whether you want to process a single file or all the open ones in the Audio File Browser (in other words, your entire project). It also gives you a last chance to select the final file format of your export, as well as a summary of the parameters of the file.

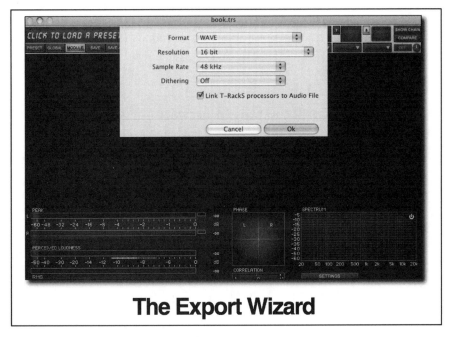

Figure 12.1 The Export wizard.

Be sure to select the correct folder where you wish the exported files to live by selecting the Browse button. Then just hit the Next button, and your export will begin processing. Note that the process is much faster than real time, unlike in some DAWs.

Hopefully you've been saving your project all along, but if not, now is the time. By saving and naming the project, T-RackS remembers everything about your project if you have to come back later to tweak it, including the list of loaded audio files, the signal chain, processor settings, and any fades or Snapshots.

Mastering for CD

Mastering for CD requires a bit more knowledge than the basics of EQ, dynamics, and editing. In fact, there are a few more steps beyond what's required for online material.

Song Order

You don't have to think about the song order much if you're planning to release your songs online, but the song order (or *sequence*) becomes important as soon as an online album, CD, or vinyl record comes into play.

The sequence of an album has become an important creative decision all on its own. In the case of a CD, a sequence that grabs the listener right at the beginning and orders the songs in such a way as to keep the listener's attention high is usually the goal, but it's a creative decision, so really anything goes. Because there are two sides to a vinyl record, a whole new set of decisions arises, since you now have two sequences to determine—one for each side.

Selecting the sequence is not normally the domain of the mastering engineer, since it's a creative decision that should be made by the producer and artist well before mastering begins.

Spreads

When mastering for CD or a vinyl record, the time in between the songs is called the *spread,* and it can be used as a creative tool just as much as the sequence of the songs. The spreads determine the pace of the album. If the songs are close together, the pace feels fast; if they're farther apart, it feels slower. Sometimes a combination of the two feels about right. Many times the spread is timed to correspond to the tempo of the previous song. In other words, if the tempo of the first song was at 123 beats per minute, the mastering engineer times the very last beat of the first song to stay in tempo with the downbeat of the next. The number of beats in between depends upon the flow of the album. Occasionally a cross-fade is used between songs so there's no real spread, but that's still a decision usually left for mastering as well.

Now, you might think that loading the songs you mastered in T-RackS back into your DAW will allow you to determine the spreads between the songs, and that will work except for one thing: You need a code embedded into the song that tells the CD when the song begins and ends (these are called *PQ codes*), and most DAWs don't have that capability. As a result, if you export the songs with the spreads, you'll get one long file, and the CD won't see it as individual songs.

Many disc burning utilities, such as Creator and Toast, allow you to insert the PQ codes, but they only have limited spread selections, usually in 0.5-second intervals. That should be enough for most situations, but if you need more precision, you'll need a dedicated PQ editor.

PQ Subcodes

PQ subcodes control the track location and running time aspects of a CD and enable the CD player to know how many tracks are present (the table of contents), where they are, how long they are, and when to change from one track to another. Editing software applications such as Audio Architect, Peak, WaveLab, and Sound Forge all have the ability to place these codes as needed.

When the CD was first developed, it had eight subcodes (labeled P to W), and there were a lot of uses intended for them that just never came to pass. Today, the only sub-codes used are P and Q. These PQ codes contain the ISRC code, the UPC code, and CD-Text. (More on these in a bit.) Most PQ editors allow a PQ log to be printed out, which is then sent with the master to the replicator as a check to ensure that the correct songs and ISRCs have been provided.

ISRC Codes

ISRC is short for *International Standard Recording Code* and is a unique identifier for each track that lists the country of origin, registrant (releasing entity, usually the label), year, and designation code (unique identifier created by the label). This code stays with the audio recording for the life of it. Even if it later appears on a compilation, the same ISRC will accompany it.

If a recording is changed in any way, it requires a new ISRC, but otherwise it will always retain the same ISRC independent of the company or format it is in. An ISRC code also may not be reused. In the US, the codes are administered by the RIAA. They can help with anti-piracy and royalty collection, though most US radio isn't very good about using the codes. There is better support for them in Europe.

Figure 12.2 shows what an ISRC looks like and what all the characters mean.

Certain circumstances can cause confusion about when to apply a new ISRC code, but most of them are covered in the following list:

■   Multiple recordings or takes of the same song produced even in the same recording session and even without any change in orchestration, arrangement, or artist require a new ISRC per recording or take.

■   A remix, different mix version, or edit mix of a song requires a new ISRC.

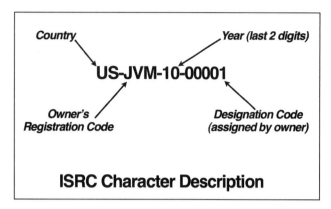

Figure 12.2   ISRC code character description.

- If the playing time changes, the song requires a new ISRC.

- Processing of historical recordings requires a new ISRC.

- Re-release as a catalog item requires a new ISRC.

- A recording sold or distributed under license by another label *uses the same* ISRC.

- A compilation where the track isn't edited or changed in any way may use the same ISRC.

So how do you get an ISRC code? If you digitally distribute your music through TuneCore or CD Baby, they'll automatically assign one for you. Many CD replicators will assign ISRCs for you, but they'll charge you a fee. That being said, it's easy enough to register yourself. Go to usisrc.org to register (it will cost a one-time fee of $75), they'll assign you a three-digit registration number, and you can begin to assign ISRC codes to all your music. Just be sure to keep a good list of the numbers and follow the rules, which are provided on the site.

UPC Code

The UPC stands for *Universal Product Code,* which is the number represented by the barcode on the back of the packaging for just about any item you buy in a store these days. UPCs are administered by the UCC, or Uniform Code Council. While an ISRC refers to a single track, the UPC code is for the entire album, and each unique physical product that is put on a store shelf has this unique code. In addition to the barcode that you find on the back of the CD package, you can actually encode this into the PQ information.

If you have any intention of selling your CD at retail and having it recorded by SoundScan for inclusion on the charts, you need a UPC. Most retailers only stock product with barcodes so they can easily keep track of them in their inventory, and SoundScan doesn't know you exist until you have a barcode. If you want to obtain a "manufacturer's number" so you can issue your own barcodes, it will cost $750 for the registration fee, but you can get a single UPC from CD Baby for $20 if you're already a member or from Nationwide Barcode (nationwidebarcode.com) for $10.

CD-Text

CD-Text information (not supported by many older CD players, and not to be confused with CDDB, which supplies titles to computer players) is included in the R through W subcodes, as are karaoke info, graphics, and other extended features not standard to the original CD spec. Most applications that allow you to insert PQ codes will also allow CD-Text info to be inserted, but it is not automatic and must be selected from a menu.

Mastering for the Internet

Although mastering used to be strictly for physical media like vinyl records and CDs, now it's just as much about online product—enough so that it deserves its own section. Let's take a look at the most common online audio file formats.

MP3 Encoding

Encoding an MP3 of your song may seem easy, but it requires a bit of thought to make it sound great, as well as some knowledge and occasionally some experimentation. Here are some tips to get you started in the right direction so you won't have to try every possible parameter combination. Remember, though, that the settings that might work on one particular song or type of music might not work on another.

Lossy Data Compression

MP3 files are encoded using what's known as *lossy* data compression. First of all, data compression is not at all like the audio compression that we've been talking about so far in this book. Data compression means decreasing the number of bits in a digital word to make the file smaller. MP3 encoding does this in a lossy manner, which means that it literally throws away certain audio information that the encoder thinks isn't important and won't be missed. Of course, if we compare an MP3 file to its original non-data compressed source file, we can usually hear a difference. That's why the following information and parameter settings are so important—so you can get the best-sounding MP3 file that sounds as close to the uncompressed source file as possible.

The Source File

Lossy data compression like MP3 makes the quality of the master mix *more* of an issue because high-quality audio will be damaged much less when using this type of MP3 encoding than low-quality source audio will. Therefore, it's vitally important that you start with the best audio quality (highest sample rate and most bits) possible. That means that sometimes it's better to start with the 24-bit master or make the MP3 while you're exporting your mix, rather than using something like a 16-bit CD master as the source for your MP3 encodes.

It's also important to listen to your encode and perhaps even try a number of different parameter settings before settling on the final product. Listen to the encode, A/B it to the original, and make any additional changes you feel necessary. Sometimes a big, thick wall of sound encodes terribly, and you need to ease back on the compression and limiting of the source track master. Other times, heavy compression can make it through the encoder better than a mix with more dynamics. There are a few predictions one can make after doing it for a while, but you can never be certain, so listening and adjusting is the only sure way.

The Encoder

Unfortunately, all MP3 encoders are not created equally, and therefore they don't provide the same quality output, so using a good encoder is the biggest advantage you can give yourself.

An MP3 encoder to consider is LAME, which is an open-source application and is an acronym for LAME Ain't an MP3 Encoder. (The name was intended to keep the developers out of legal trouble during the early days of digital music.) The consensus seems to be that LAME and the Fraunhofer encoder (Fraunhofer was part of a consortium of companies who invented the MP3 format) produce the highest-quality MP3 files for average bit rates of 128 kbs and higher. Another good MP3 encoder is the one found inside iTunes.

Bit Rate.   Regardless of the encoder, there's one parameter that matters the most in determining the quality of the encode, and that's bit rate, which is the number of bits of encoded data that are used to represent each second of audio. Lossy encoders, such as MP3, provide a number of different options for bit rate. Typically, the rates chosen are between 128 and 320 kilobits per second (kbs). By contrast, uncompressed audio as stored on a compact disc has a bit rate of about 1400 kbs.

MP3 files encoded with a lower bit rate will result in a smaller file and therefore will download faster, but they generally play back at a lower quality. With a bit rate too low, *compression artifacts* (in other words, sounds that were not present in the original recording) may appear in the reproduction. A good demonstration of compression artifacts is provided by the sound of applause, which is hard to data compress because it's random. As a result, the failings of an encoder are more obvious and become audible as a slight ringing.

Conversely, a high bit rate encode will almost always produce a better-sounding file, but this also results in a larger file, which may take an unacceptable amount of storage space or time to download (although in these days of seemingly unlimited storage and widespread high-speed Internet, that's becoming less and less of a factor).

Bit Rate Settings.   For average signals with good encoders, many listeners once considered a bit rate of 128 kbs (providing a compression ratio of approximately 11:1) to be near enough to compact disc quality. However, listening tests show that with a bit of practice, many listeners can reliably distinguish 128-kbs MP3s from CD originals.

When that happens, many times they reconsider and then deem the 128-kbs MP3 audio to be of unacceptably low quality. Yet other listeners, and the same listeners in other environments (such as in a noisy moving vehicle or at a party), will consider the quality quite acceptable. That being said, 160 kbs has mostly become the norm for acceptable-quality MP3s. Here are the pros and cons of the different bit rates.

- **128 kbs.** Lowest acceptable bit rate, but may have marginal quality depending upon the encoder. Results in some artifacts but small file size.

- **160 kbs.** Lowest bit rate considered usable for a high-quality file.

- **320 kbs.** The highest quality, large file size, but may be indistinguishable from CD.

Constant versus Average versus Variable Bit Rate.   There are three modes that are coupled to bit rate that have a bearing on the final sound quality of the encode.

- **Variable Bit Rate (VBR) mode.** Maintains a constant quality while raising and lowering the bit rate depending upon how complex the program is. Size is less predictable than with ABR (see below), but the quality is usually better.

- **Average Bit Rate (ABR) mode.** Varies the bit rate around a specified target bit rate.

- **Constant Bit Rate (CBR) mode.** Maintains a steady bit rate regardless of the complexity of the program. CBR mode usually provides the lowest-quality encode, but the file size is very predictable.

At a given bit rate range, VBR will provide higher quality than ABR, which will provide higher quality than CBR. The exception to this is when you choose the highest possible bit rate of 320 kbs, where, depending upon the encoder, the mode may have little bearing on the final sound quality.

Other Settings.   There are some additional parameter settings that can have a huge influence on the quality of the final encode. These include:

- **Mid-Side Joint Stereo (sometimes called MS Joint Stereo).** Encodes all of the common audio on one channel and the difference audio (stereo minus the mono information) on the other channel. This is intended for low bit rate material to retain surround information from a surround mix source and is not needed or desired for stereo source files. *Do not select under normal circumstances.*

- **Intensity Joint Stereo.** Again intended for lower bit rates, Intensity Joint Stereo combines the left and right channels by saving some frequencies as mono and placing them in the stereo field based on the intensity of the sound. This should not be used if the stereo audio contains surround-encoded material.

- **Stereo Narrowing.** Again intended for lower bit rates, allows narrowing of the stereo signal to increase overall sound quality.

It's better not to check any of these parameters when encoding stereo files that originate at 16-bit or above. With these disabled, the encoding will remain in true stereo, with all of the information from the original left channel going to the left side, and the same for the right channel.

MP3 Encoding Tips

If you want the best-sounding MP3s possible, follow these tips:

- Start with the highest quality audio file possible.

- Filter out the top end at whatever frequency works best. (Judge by ear.) MP3 has the most difficulty with high frequencies—rolling them off liberates a lot of processing for encoding the lower and mid frequencies. You trade some top end for better quality in the rest of the spectrum.

- A busy mix can lose punch after encoding. Sparse mixes, such as acoustic jazz trios, seem to retain more of the original audio punch.

- Use Variable Bit Rate.

- Turn *off* Mid-Side Joint Stereo, Intensity Joint Stereo, and Stereo Narrowing.

- Try not to use a bit rate below 160 kbs. (Higher is better.)

- Don't hyper-compress. Leave some dynamic range so the encoding algorithm has something to look at.

- Use multiband compression or other dynamic spectral effects very sparingly. They just confuse the encoding algorithm.

- Set your encoder for maximum quality, which allows it to process for best results. The encoding time is negligible anyway.

- Remember, MP3 encoding almost always results in the post-encoded material being slightly hotter than the original material. Limit the output of the material intended for MP3 to −1.1 dB, instead of the commonly used −0.1 or −0.2 dB, so you don't get digital overs.

Exporting for iTunes

iTunes uses the AAC (*Advanced Audio Coding*) file format as a standard for the music in its store and, contrary to popular belief, it's not a proprietary format owned by Apple. In fact, it's part of the MP4 specification and generally delivers excellent-quality files that are about 30 percent smaller than a standard MP3 of the same data rate. All new music destined for the iTunes store must be encoded at 256 kbs at a constant bit rate with a 44.1-kHz sample rate. The iTunes store stopped selling 128-kbs songs in April 2008.

Here's some info on some of the parameters of the AAC encoder.

- **Stereo Bit Rate.** This allows you to select the bit rate. The standard setting is now 256 kbps, and the highest-quality setting for this format is 320 kbps.

- **Sample Rate.** This enables you to select the sample rate. Never use a higher sample rate than the rate used for the source. (In other words, don't use 48 kHz if your source was 44.1 kHz.) Doing so will make the file larger without you gaining anything in terms of quality.

- **Variable Bit Rate Encoding (VBR).** This option helps keep file size down, but the audio quality might be affected. VBR varies the number of bits used to store the music depending on the complexity of the sound. If you select the Highest setting from the Quality pop-up menu for VBR, iTunes encodes up to the maximum bit rate of 320 kbps in sections of songs where the sound is complex enough to require a high bit rate. Meanwhile, iTunes keeps the rest of the song at a lower bit rate to save file space. The lower limit is set by the rate that you select in the Stereo Bit Rate pop-up menu.

- **Channels.** This pop-up menu enables you to choose how you want the music to play through speakers—in stereo or mono. Select the Auto setting to have iTunes use the appropriate setting for the music.

- **Optimize for Voice.** This option is meant for podcasters and filters the audio to favor the human voice, which is obviously not something you'd want for music.

It's best to select the highest bit rate in the Stereo Bit Rate pop-up menu and leave the other two pop-up menus set to Auto.

FLAC Files

A format that's recently gotten a lot of attention is the lossless FLAC (*Free Lossless Audio Codec*) format. It works somewhat the same as a standard MP3 file; only it's lossless, like a zip file, and designed specifically for audio. Unlike other lossless codecs by DTS and Dolby, FLAC is also non-proprietary, is unencumbered by patents, and has open-source implementation. What's more, FLAC has been adopted as a release format of choice by some of the world's biggest recording artists, from Pearl Jam to Nine Inch Nails to the Eagles, and even reissues from the Beatles.

FLAC supports up to eight channels. You don't need to specify a bit rate because it automatically determines it, and it has a "cue sheet" metadata block for storing CD table of contents, track, and index points. It's an excellent way to deliver the highest fidelity music file with a reasonably small file size, but it's not yet supported by all applications or players.

Although FLAC files aren't supported by T-RackS 3, there are a number of players and encoders that can be downloaded for free, as well as QuickTime playback components and iTunes scripts.

ALAC Files

The Apple Lossless Audio Codec is Apple's version of FLAC. It is a variation of the MP4 specification and is designated with an .m4a filename extension. Like FLAC, it compresses a file to about half of its original size and can support multiple channels and sample rates, as well as 16- or 24-bit depths. An ALAC encoder is built into iTunes and can be accessed from the Preferences menu under Import Settings.

Summary Questions

You can find answers to the Summary Questions in the Appendix at the end of this book.

1. What is an album sequence?

2. What are spreads?

3. What are PQ subcodes?

4. Why can't you just export your songs for a CD from your typical DAW if they're placed on a single timeline?

5. What is an ISRC code?

6. How can you obtain an ISRC code for your songs?

7. List three instances where a new ISRC code is required for the same song.

8. What's a UPC code?

9. How can you obtain a UPC code for your album?

10. What is lossy data compression?

Glossary

0 dB Full Scale. The highest level that can be recorded in the digital domain. Recording beyond 0 dB FS results in severe distortion.

AAC. Advanced Audio Coding is a standard lossy compression encoding scheme for digital audio used exclusively on Apple iTunes.

A/D. Analog-to-digital converter. This device converts the analog waveform into the digital language that can be used by a digital audio workstation.

AIFF. Audio Interchange File Format (also known as *Apple Interchange File Format*) is an audio file format designed for use in the Apple Macintosh operating system but is now used in PCs as well.

airplay. When a song gets played on the radio.

ambience. The background noise of an environment.

asset. A multimedia element—either sound, picture, graphic, or text.

attack. The first part of a sound. On a compressor/limiter, a control that affects how that device will respond to the attack of a sound.

attenuation. A decrease in level.

Augspurger. George Augspurger of Perception Inc. in Los Angeles is one of the most revered studio designers. He also designs large studio monitors, each having dual 15-inch woofers and a horn tweeter.

automation. A system that memorizes and then plays back the position of all faders, mutes on a console, and just about every parameter in a DAW.

bandwidth. The number of frequencies that a device will pass before the signal degrades. A human being can supposedly hear from 20 Hz to 20 kHz, so the bandwidth of the human ear is 20 Hz to 20 kHz. Sometimes applies to computer data rate, where a high rate per second represents a wider bandwidth.

bar code. A series of vertical bars of varying widths in which the numbers zero through nine are represented by a different pattern of bars that can be read by a laser scanner.

Bar codes are commonly found on consumer products and are used for inventory control, and in the case of CDs, to tally sales.

big ears. The ability to be very aware of everything going on within the session and with the music. The ability to rapidly dissect a track in terms of key and arrangement.

bit rate. The transmission rate of a digital system.

bottom. Bass frequencies, the lower end of the audio spectrum. *See also* low end.

brickwall. A limiter employing look-ahead technology that is so efficient that the signal will never exceed a certain predetermined level and there will be no digital overs.

buss. A signal pathway.

catalog. Older albums or recordings under control of the record label.

clip. To overload and cause distortion.

clipping. When an audio signal begins to distort because a circuit in the signal path is overloaded, the top of the waveform becomes "clipped" off and begins to look square instead of rounded. This usually results in some type of distortion, which can be either soft and barely noticeable or horribly crunchy-sounding.

color. To affect the timbral qualities of a sound.

comb filter. A distortion produced by combining an electronic or acoustic signal with a delayed copy of itself. The result is peaks and dips introduced into the frequency response.

competitive level. A mix level that is as loud as your competitor's mix.

compression. Signal processing that controls and evens out the dynamics of a sound.

compressor. A signal-processing device used to compress audio dynamics.

cross-fade. In mastering, when one song is fading out and another is fading in at the same time.

cut. To decrease, attenuate, or make less.

cutter head. The assembly on a vinyl cutting lathe that holds the cutting stylus between a set of drive coils powered by very high-powered (typically 1,000 to 3,500 watts) amplifiers.

D/A. Digital-to-analog converter. This device converts the digital 1s and 0s back to an analog waveform.

data compression. A process that uses a specially designed algorithm to decrease the number of bits in a file for more efficient storage and transmission.

DAW. A digital audio workstation. A computer loaded with recording software that is connected to an input/output interface box.

dB. Stands for *decibel,* which is a unit of measurement of sound level or loudness.

decay. The time it takes for a signal to fall below audibility.

decoupling. Isolating speakers from a desk or console by using rubber or carpet.

digital domain. When a signal source is converted into a series of electronic pulses represented by 1s and 0s, the signal is then in the digital domain.

digital overs. The point beyond 0 on a digital processor where the red Over indicator lights, resulting in a digital overload.

dither. A low-level noise signal used to gradually reduce the length of a digital word.

DJ. Disc jockey. A term used for the on-air radio person who played the records that the station was broadcasting. Later replaced by the on-air "personality."

dynamic range. A ratio that describes the difference between the loudest and the quietest audio. The higher the number, equaling the greater dynamic range, the better.

edgy. A sound with an abundance of midrange frequencies.

element. A component or ingredient of the mix.

EQ. Equalizer, or to adjust the equalizers (tone controls) to affect the timbral balance of a sound.

equalization. Adjustment of the frequency spectrum to even out or alter tonal imbalances.

equalizer. A tone control that can vary in sophistication from very simple to very complex. *See also* parametric equalizer.

feather. Rather than applying a large amount of equalization at a single frequency, small amounts are added at the frequencies adjoining the one of principle concern instead.

FLAC. Free Lossless Audio Codec. A lossless file format used to make digital audio files smaller in size, yet they suffer no degradation of audio quality.

Fletcher-Munson curves. A set of measurements that describes how the frequency response of the ear changes at different sound pressure levels. For instance, we generally hear very high and very low frequencies much better as the overall sound pressure level is increased.

gain. The amount a sound is boosted.

gain reduction. The amount of compression or limiting.

gain-staging. Adjusting the gain of each stage of the signal chain so the output of one doesn't overload the input of another.

groove. The pulse of the song and how the instruments dynamically breathe with it. Or, the part of a vinyl record that contains the mechanical information that is transferred to electronic info by the stylus.

headroom. The amount of dynamic range between the normal operating level and the maximum output level, which is usually the onset of clipping.

hertz. A measurement unit of audio frequency, meaning the number of cycles per second. High numbers represent high sounds, and low numbers represent low sounds.

high-pass filter. An electronic device that allows the high frequencies to pass while attenuating the low frequencies. Used to eliminate low-frequency artifacts such as hum and rumble. The frequency point where it cuts off is usually either switchable or variable.

hyper-compression. Too much buss compression during mixing or limiting during mastering in an effort to make the recording louder results in what's known as *hyper-compression,* a condition that essentially leaves no dynamics and makes the track sound lifeless.

Hz. Short for hertz.

I/O. The input/output of a device.

ISRC code. An international standard code for uniquely identifying sound recordings and music video recordings. An ISRC code identifies a particular recording, not the song itself; therefore, different recordings, edits, and remixes of the same song will each have their own ISRC codes.

kbs. Kilobits per second. The amount of digital information sent per second. Sometimes referred to as *bandwidth.*

kHz. 1,000 Hertz (for example, 4 kHz = 4,000 Hz).

knee. How quickly a compressor will turn on once it reaches the threshold. A soft knee turns on gradually and is less audible than a hard knee.

latency. Latency is a measure of the time it takes (in milliseconds) for your audio signal to pass through your system during the recording process. This delay is caused by the time it takes for your computer to receive, understand, process, and send the signal back to your outputs.

limiter. A signal-processing device used to constrict or reduce audio dynamics, reducing the loudest peaks in volume.

look-ahead. In a mastering limiter, look-ahead processing delays the audio signal a small amount (about 2 milliseconds or so) so that the limiter can anticipate the peaks in such a way that it catches the peak before it gets by.

lossless compression. A compression format that recovers all the original data from the compressed version and suffers no degradation of audio quality as a result. FLAC and ALAC are lossless compression schemes.

lossy compression. A digital file compression format that cannot recover all of its original data from the compressed version. Supposedly, some of what is normally recorded before compression is imperceptible, with the louder sounds masking the softer ones. As a result, some data can be eliminated since it's not heard anyway. This selective approach, determined by extensive psychoacoustic research, is the basis for lossy compression. MP3 and AAC are lossy compression schemes.

low end. The lower end of the audio spectrum, or bass frequencies usually below 200 Hz.

low-pass filter. An electronic frequency filter that allows only the low frequencies to pass while attenuating the high frequencies. The frequency point where it cuts off is usually either switchable or variable.

LPCM. Linear Pulse Code Modulation. This is the most common method of digital encoding of audio used today and is the same digital encoding method used on current audio CDs. In LPCM, the analog waveform is measured at discrete points in time and converted into a digital representation.

makeup gain. A control on a compressor/limiter that applies additional gain to the signal. This is required since the signal is automatically decreased when the compressor is working. Makeup gain "makes up" the gain and brings it back to where it was prior to being compressed.

mastering. The process of turning a collection of songs into a record by making them sound like they belong together in tone, volume, and timing (spacing between songs).

metadata. Data that describes the primary data. For instance, metadata can be data about an audio file that indicates the date recorded, sample rate, resolution, and so on.

midrange. Middle frequencies starting from around 250 Hz up to 4,000 Hz.

modeling. Developing a software algorithm that is an electronic representation of the sound of a hardware audio device down to the smallest behaviors and nuances.

monaural. A mix that contains a single channel and usually comes from only one speaker.

mono. Short for monaural, or single audio playback channel.

MP3. The de facto standard data compression format used to make audio files smaller in size.

multiband compression. A compressor that is able to individually compress different frequency bands as a means of having more control over the compression process.

mute. An on/off switch. To mute something would mean to turn it off.

native resolution. The sample rate and bit depth of a distribution container. For example, the native resolution of a CD is 44.1 kHz and 16 bits. The native resolution in film work is 48 kHz and 24 bits.

normalization. A selection on a DAW that looks for the highest peak of an audio file and adjusts all the levels of the file upward to match that level.

out of phase. The polarity of two channels (it could be the left and right channels of a stereo program) are reversed, thereby causing the center of the program (such as the vocal) to diminish in level. Electronically, when one cable is wired backwards from all the others.

overs. Digital overs occur when the level is so high that it tries to go beyond 0 dB Full Scale on a typical digital level meter found in almost all equipment. A red Overload indicator usually will turn on, accompanied by the crunchy, distorted sound of waveform clipping.

pan. Short for panorama, this indicates the left and right position of an instrument within the stereo spectrum.

panning. Moving a sound across the stereo spectrum.

parametric equalizer. A tone control where the gain, frequency, and bandwidth are all variable.

peak. A sound that's temporarily much higher than the sound surrounding it.

phantom image. In a stereo system, if the signal is of equal strength in the left and right channels, the resultant sound appears to come from in between them. This is a phantom image.

phase. The relationship between two separate sound signals when combined into one.

phase meter. A dedicated meter that displays the relative phase of a stereo signal.

phase shift. The process during which some frequencies (usually those below 100 Hz) are slowed down ever so slightly as they pass through a device. This is usually exaggerated by excessive use of equalization and is highly undesirable.

plug-in. An add-on to a computer application that adds functionality to it. EQ, modulation, and reverb are examples of DAW plug-ins.

PQ codes. Subcodes included along with the main data channel as a means of placing control data, such as start IDs and tables of contents on a CD.

pre-delay. The time between the dry sound and the onset of reverberation. The correct setting of the pre-delay parameter can make a difference in the clarity of the mix.

presence. Accentuated upper midrange frequencies (anywhere from 5 to 10 kHz).

producer. The equivalent of a movie director, the producer has the ability to craft the songs of an artist or a band technically, sonically, and musically.

proximity effect. The inherent low-frequency boost that occurs with a directional microphone as it gets closer to the signal source.

Pultec. An equalizer sold during the '50s and '60s by Western Electric that is highly prized today for its smooth, unique sound.

pumping. When the level of a mix increases and then decreases noticeably. Pumping is caused by the improper setting of the attack and release times on a compressor.

punchy. A description for a quality of sound that infers good reproduction of dynamics with a strong impact. The term sometimes means emphasis in the 200 Hz and 5 kHz areas.

Q. The bandwidth, or the frequency range of a filter or an equalizer.

ratio. A parameter control on a compressor/limiter that determines how much compression or limiting will occur when the signal exceeds threshold.

record. A generic term for the distribution method of a recording. Regardless of whether it's a CD, vinyl, or a digital file, it is still known as a record.

reference level. This is the audio level, either electronic or acoustic, to which a sound system is aligned.

release. The last part of a sound. On a compressor/limiter, a control that affects how that device will respond to the release of a sound.

resonance. *See* resonant frequency.

resonant frequency. A particular frequency or band of frequencies that is accentuated, usually due to some extraneous acoustic, electronic, or mechanical factor.

return. Inputs on a recording console especially dedicated for effects devices, such as reverbs and delays. The return inputs are usually not as sophisticated as normal channel inputs on a console.

RIAA. Recording Industry Association of America. A trade organization for record labels.

roll-off. Usually another word for high-pass filter, although it can refer to a low-pass filter as well.

sample rate. The rate at which the analog waveform is measured. The more samples per second of the analog waveform that are taken, the better digital representation of the waveform that occurs, resulting in greater bandwidth for the signal.

scope. Short for *oscilloscope,* an electronic measurement device that produces a picture of the audio waveform.

sequencing. Setting the order in which the songs will play on a CD or vinyl record.

shelving curve. A type of equalizer circuit used to boost or cut a signal above or below a specified frequency. Usually the high- and low-band equalizers built into many mixing boards are the shelving type.

sibilance. A short burst of high frequencies in a vocal due to heavy compression, resulting in the S sounds being overemphasized.

sound field. The direct listening area.

SoundScan. The company (a division of Nielsen Company) that measures record sales. Whenever a CD or DVD is sold, the barcode on the unit is scanned and recorded by SoundScan.

source. An original master that is not a copy or a clone.

spectrum. The complete audible range of audio signals.

SPL. Sound pressure level.

spread. The time in between songs on a CD or vinyl record.

stems. Mixes that have their major elements broken out separately for individual adjustment at a later time.

sub. Short for subwoofer.

subwoofer. A low-frequency speaker with a frequency response from about 25 Hz to 120 Hz.

tempo. The rate of speed that a song is played.

threshold. The point at which an effect takes place. On a compressor/limiter, for instance, the Threshold control adjusts the point at which compression will begin.

timbre. Tonal color.

trim. A control that sets the gain of a device, or the process of reducing the size or playing time of an audio file.

track. A term sometimes used to mean a song. In recording, a separate musical performance that is recorded.

transformer. An electronic component that either matches or changes impedance. Transformers are large, heavy, and expensive but are in part responsible for the desirable sound in vintage audio gear.

tube. Short for *vacuum tube,* an electronic component used as the primary amplification device in most vintage audio gear. Equipment utilizing vacuum tubes runs hot, is heavy, and has a short life, but it has a desirable sound.

TV mix. A mix without the vocals so the artist can sing live to the backing tracks during a television appearance.

unity gain. When the output level of a process or processor exactly matches its input level.

WAV. A WAV file is an audio data file developed by the IBM and Microsoft corporations and is the PC equivalent of an AIFF file. It is identified by the .wav file extension.

word length. The number of bits in a word. Word length is in groups of eight. The longer the word length, the better the dynamic range.

Appendix : Answers to Summary Questions

Chapter 1

1. What are the three categories of mix preparation?

    The three categories are technical prep (where you prep the audio files that will be used in the session for mixing), setup prep (where you prep the session file itself for mixing), and physical prep (where you prepare yourself personally for mixing).

2. Why is it important to make a copy of your session and rename it while prepping?

    You want to make a copy of your session so you have a backup in case you ever have to go back to it for any reason.

3. Why is editing the timing of a track by eye dangerous?

    Editing the timing of a region or a track by eye is dangerous because what looks correct may not sound that way when you play it back. It's best to edit more by listening than by looking at the edit.

4. List four concerns when tweaking the timing of a track.

    Every beat doesn't have to be perfect. (It can suck the life out of a performance if it is.) Make sure you listen against the drums. (It's easier to hear whether your edits work.) Be careful with the bass. (It might speak better if it's slightly behind the kick.) Be sure to trim the releases. (It will make everything sound tighter.)

5. How do you tighten up the releases of a track?

    To tighten the releases, trim the fade or end of a phrase so it's the same length as all the other phrases of a section.

6. What's the reason for eliminating the various noises of a track?

    Eliminating the noises of a track will make it sound a lot cleaner and more distinct.

7. List five preparation items for setup.

Any five of the following setup prep items will work: Make a copy of the session, delete any tracks that are empty, deactivate and hide any tracks that you're not using, arrange the track order so like instruments are grouped together, color-code the tracks so they're easy to find, insert section markers to find parts of the song quickly, label the tracks so you don't mistake one for another, set up groups so the mix is easier, set up your effects to save time later, assign the channels to groups or effects, and set up your compressors and limiters on channels that you know will need them so you don't have to break your concentration to set them up later.

8. If you're not using a track, why should it be deactivated and hidden?

You want to deactivate and hide an unused track to decrease the processor load, to unclutter the view of the session, and to make sure that you don't mistake it for another channel.

9. Why are section markers so useful?

Section markers make it easy to quickly find a section of the song.

10. Why are mix groups so useful?

By grouping things such as the drums and background vocals, you make them easier to balance against the other instruments, and it gives you the ability to compress the entire group if necessary.

Chapter 2

1. What are three reasons why the monitor speakers that your favorite mixer uses might not work for you?

Everyone is unique in the way they hear, so choosing a monitor because someone else uses it isn't a good idea. You probably hear differently than the other mixer, what works in his room might not work in yours, and the type of music that you work on might be different.

2. How do you evaluate a monitor?

To evaluate a pair of monitor speakers you have to listen to see how even the frequency balance is (to see whether one frequency range is accentuated or attenuated over the others), you want to make sure that the frequency balance stays the same at any playback level, and you want to make sure that you can get enough playback level without distortion to fit your needs.

3. How far apart should the speakers be placed?

The speakers should generally be placed as far apart as you are from the monitors. That being said, some room tuners and studio designers feel that 67.5 inches is a "magic" distance.

4. What happens if they're too close together? Too far apart?

    If the monitors are too close together, your stereo field will be smeared, and you'll lose spatial definition. If they're too far apart, the focal point will be too far behind the mixer's head.

5. What is the monitor focal point?

    The focal point is the "sweet spot," or the place in the room where the sound of each monitor intersects with the other.

6. Why is it located at a point just behind the mixer's head?

    If the focal point is located behind the mixer's head, the stereo field is widened, and some of the hype of the speaker (if it has any) may be decreased a little.

7. Why is decoupling the monitors so important?

    Decoupling, or isolating the monitors from a desk, stand, or meter bridge, eliminates any comb filtering or phase cancelation due to the sound from a hard surface, such as a desk, hitting your ear before the sound in the air from the speaker does.

8. What are two ways to decouple monitors?

    Two ways to decouple monitors are to use a piece of soft neoprene rubber, such as a mouse pad, or to use a commercial product, such as the Primacoustic Recoil Stabilizers.

9. Why is sustained listening at high volume levels not recommended?

    Exposure to high volume levels for long periods of time may cause physical damage to your ears, will probably cause listener fatigue so you won't be able to work as long, and will cause you to have a more difficult time finding the correct balance between the instruments in the mix.

10. Why is a lot of mixing done at quiet levels?

    Many mixers prefer to mix at quiet levels because they can hear the balance between the instruments and vocals better.

Chapter 3

1. What does a compressor do?

    A compressor is an automated level control that uses the input level to determine the output level. It controls the dynamics of an audio signal by lifting the level of the soft passages and lowering the level of the loud ones so there's less difference between them.

2.   What does a gain ratio of 6:1 mean?

A gain ratio set to 6:1 means that for every 6 dB of input signal, there will only be 1 dB of signal output.

3.   Give two situations where you might use a compressor.

Two common uses for a compressor would be on a kick drum where a drummer doesn't hit each beat with the same intensity or on a vocal where the singer doesn't sing every word or phrase at the same level.

4.   What can happen if you set the attack of a compressor too fast?

If you set the attack time of a compressor too fast, you can eliminate the transients from a sound, making it dull and lifeless.

5.   What can happen if you set the release of a compressor too fast?

If you set the release time of a compressor too fast, you can cause it to quickly reduce the signal and then have it quickly go back to its original volume level, causing the sound to seem to pump.

6.   Describe how to set up a compressor.

To adjust a compressor to operate properly, start with the slowest attack time and the fastest release time. Then turn the attack time faster until the signal just begins to dull and turn the release time slower so its volume breathes in time with the pulse of the music.

7.   What's the difference between a compressor and a limiter?

A compressor is used to even out the signal level, raising the parts that are low in level and decreasing the points where the level is too high, while a limiter mostly decreases the level, allowing it to reach a predetermined point and little more.

8.   At what compression ratio does a compressor become a limiter?

A compressor is considered a limiter once the gain ratio reaches a 10:1 setting.

9.   List three instances where a limiter would be used instead of a compressor.

A limiter can be found in sound reinforcement systems to keep the transients from overdriving speakers, at the end of an audio signal chain at a radio or television station so it doesn't exceed its assigned transmission level, or in a mastering chain to keep the signal from overloading.

10.   At what level is the Output Ceiling control usually set on the Brickwall Limiter?

The Output Ceiling control on the Brickwall Limiter is usually set at −0.1 or −0.2 dB to keep the level hot, yet keep it from overloading.

Chapter 4

1.   What are the primary goals of equalizing?

Equalization is used to make an instrument sound clearer or more defined, make an instrument or mix larger than life, or make instruments in a mix fit together better.

2.   What are the six major frequency bands?

The six major frequency bands are the sub-bass band (16 to 60 Hz), the bass band (60 to 250 Hz), the low-mid band (250 Hz to 2 kHz), the high-mid band (2 to 4 kHz), the presence band (4 to 6 kHz), and the brilliance band (6 to 16 kHz).

3.   Which frequency band can cause listener fatigue if emphasized too much?

The low-mid band (250 Hz to 2 kHz) can cause the listener to become fatigued if emphasized too much.

4.   Which frequency band can cause the "m," "b," and "v" voice sounds to be masked if emphasized too much?

The high-mid band (2 to 4 kHz) is chiefly responsible for the clarity of the "m," "b," and "v" voice sounds. Too much emphasis of this band can decrease the clarity of these sounds.

5.   Which frequency band can cause the music to seem closer to the listener when boosted?

Boosting the presence band (4 to 6 kHz) can make the listener feel as if the music is closer to him.

6.   Which frequency band can cause vocal sibilance if emphasized too much?

The brilliance band (6 to 16 kHz) can cause vocal sibilance if emphasized too much.

7.   The more instruments in the mix, the _smaller_ each has to be for everything to fit together. The fewer instruments in a mix, the bigger they can be frequency-wise.

8.   What is subtractive equalization?

Subtractive equalization occurs when frequencies are mostly attenuated (subtracted) instead of boosting them on an equalizer.

9.   Why is subtractive equalization used?

Subtractive equalization many times works better than boosting because it causes a track to blend better with the others in a mix, since any phase shift caused by the process of equalization is decreased.

10.   Where are the two spots in the frequency spectrum that subtractive equalization is most effective?

Subtractive equalization is most effective between 400 to 600 Hz and 2 and 4 kHz because these are two areas of the frequency spectrum that a directional microphone frequently emphasizes.

Chapter 5

1.   Why did the use of buss compression begin?

The use of mix buss compression started when artists began to demand that their mixes sound more like the finished product that they were hearing on the radio. Buss compression was inserted by the mixing engineer to more closely simulate what it would sound like after mastering.

2.   What is a client mix?

A client mix is a compressed mix that simulates a mastered mix that is given only to the client. The final mix that eventually goes to mastering may contain much less compression so the mastering engineer has more to work with.

3.   What are the advantages of inserting a mix buss compressor toward the end of your mix?

When a mix buss compressor is inserted toward the end of a mix, if you don't like the sound you can easily replace the compressor for another without altering the balance of the mix.

4.   What are the advantages of inserting a mix buss compressor at the beginning of your mix?

An advantage of inserting a mix buss compressor at the start of a mix is that the "glue" that a buss compressor brings to a mix is heard from the beginning, so a mix may come together a little more quickly. The mixer also has more control over the total compression of a mix, so it is easier to increase or decrease it as the client would like. Finally, adding the buss compression at the beginning of the mix evens out the level of many of the lead instruments, so that the mix may require less level automation as a result.

5.   What are the disadvantages of inserting a mix buss compressor at the beginning of your mix?

When a mix buss compressor is inserted at the beginning of a mix, if you decide that you don't like its sound when you're finished, it's difficult to replace it with another model, because the balance will be altered.

6. What is an alternative to buss compression?

    An alternative to buss compression is individually compressing any subgroups that may be assigned.

7. What is a stems mix?

    A stems mix breaks down each individual mix element into its own subgroup in order to have more control over the final balance of the mix.

8. What's the best way to set up a buss compressor to get a punchy track?

    To adjust a compressor to make the sound punchy, first start with the snare drum to use as a reference. Begin listening with the slowest attack time and the fastest release time on the compressor, then turn the attack time faster until the sound of the snare drum just begins to dull, then turn the release time slower until its volume comes back to 90 to 100 percent of normal. Add the rest of the mix back in and make any adjustments from there as necessary.

9. What happens if the attack time is set too fast on a buss compressor?

    Attack times that are set too fast will reduce how punchy the track sounds because the transients of the song are decreased.

10. What happens if the release time is set too fast on a buss compressor?

    Release times that are set too fast will cause the track to pump out of time with the song.

Chapter 6

1. What is mixing in the box?

    Mixing in the box means doing a mix completely inside a computer a DAW application instead of using a traditional recording console.

2. What's the greatest advantage of mixing in the box?

    The greatest advantage of mixing in the box is the fact that every parameter of every track and effect is instantly recallable to just where you left it last.

3. What's the average amount of time that a mixer likes when using a console?

    Most mixers like to have about a day and a half to complete a mix using a console.

4. List five ways that you know your mix is finished.

    The mix of a song can be considered finished when the groove of the song is solid, you can distinctly hear every instrument, every lyric and every note of every line or solo can be heard clearly, the mix has punch, the mix has a focal point, the mix has contrast, all noises and glitches have been eliminated, and you can play your mix up against songs that you love and it sounds as good.

5. What is an up mix?

An up mix is a separate alternative mix from the master mix, in which the level of the lead vocal or instrument is increased by a small amount, usually from 0.5 to 1 dB.

6. List two ways that alternate mixes may come in handy.

You can cut and paste a piece of an alternate mix into your main mix to fix a word that you can't hear, substitute another part of the song that's louder or softer, or splice out objectionable lyrics.

7. Give three examples of alternative mixes.

Some possible alternative mixes include the album version, album version with vocals up, edited single version, Contemporary Hits Radio version, Album-Oriented Radio version, Adult Contemporary Radio version, and TV mix, among others.

8. What is a TV mix?

A TV mix is a complete mix minus the lead vocal or lead instrument that allows the artist to perform on television with a live vocal against the mixed backing tracks of the song.

9. Why is mono compatibility of the mix so important?

Mono compatibility of the mix is important because when an out-of-phase mix is played back in mono, anything in the center of the mix, such as vocals or lead instruments, may be cancelled out and may not be heard in the playback.

10. Why are hot mix levels not important to give to mastering?

Hot mix levels are not important to give to the mastering engineer because the mastering engineer can usually do a better job at getting the level up to a competitive commercial level than the mixing engineer can.

Chapter 7

1. What is mastering?

Mastering is the process of turning a collection of songs into a record by making them sound as if they belong together in tone, volume, and timing (spacing between songs).

2.   List two examples of when you need mastering.

You need mastering if you have a song that has a softer level than another, sounds dull or bright compared to another song, or sounds too bottom heavy or bottom light compared to another song.

3.   List two differences between a pro and an amateur.

A pro generally has better gear, especially the monitors and listening environment; he has more experience in knowing what sounds good and what doesn't; and he always makes a backup of everything he does.

4.   What are you trying to accomplish by mastering?

You're trying to make a group of songs sound the same in tonal quality and level, but also you are trying to make them as loud as other commercially released songs. You then want to finish them off by editing out any count-offs, glitches, or noises; fixing the fades if necessary; and adding PQ and ISRC codes and spreads between songs for a CD or vinyl record release.

5.   What is an SDII file?

SDII (Sound Designer 2) is an audio file format introduced by Digidesign in the early days of workstations. The format is no longer widely used.

6.   What is a CAF file?

CAF stands for Core Audio File and is an audio file format developed by Apple in an effort to overcome some of the limitations of the older WAV and AIFF formats.

7.   What are three advantages of the CAF format?

CAF files don't have the 4-GB limit of other formats. They can hold any type of audio or metadata, any number of audio channels, and auxiliary information such as text annotations, markers, channel layouts, and other types of DAW data. It's also possible to append new data to the end of the file.

8.   What file resolution is required for CD, online, and video?

The file resolution required for CD, online, and video is 16 bits.

9.   What is gained by exporting a file at a higher resolution than you started with?

You gain nothing by exporting a file at a higher resolution than you started with, plus your file size is larger.

10.   What is the sample rate for film and television?

The sample rate for film and television is 48 kHz.

Chapter 8

1. What are the greatest impediments to doing your own mastering?

   The greatest impediments to doing your own mastering are your monitoring system and monitoring environment, because most monitors don't provide a wide enough frequency response (especially on the low end), and the environment is not built for monitoring or mastering.

2. Why is mastering on the same monitors you mixed on not a good idea?

   Mastering on the same monitors you mixed on is not a good idea because you will compound any of the frequency problems that the monitors might have that you imparted on your mix.

3. What's the most important thing to do before you begin to master?

   The most important thing you can do before you begin to master is to listen to recordings and CDs of other songs that you like the sound of so you have a reference point to start from.

4. Why should you limit your listening to only two different levels?

   If you listen at varying levels, your reference point will be thrown off, and it will be difficult to make decisions on any small changes that you may make.

5. Why is a second set of monitors necessary for mastering?

   You need to listen on a second set of monitors so you're sure that your mastering will translate to different types of playback monitors.

6. What is the primary ingredient in mastering?

   The primary ingredient in mastering is your ears!

7. How do you prevent yourself from over- or under-EQing?

   You prevent yourself from over- or under-EQing by listening to CDs or recordings of material that you think sounds great before you begin mastering, so you have a reference point.

Chapter 9

1. What's the difference between a peak meter and a VU meter?

   The VU meter reads the average level of the audio signal and has a relatively slow response. The peak meter reads the peaks of the audio signal and has a very fast response.

2.   What does VU stand for?

VU stands for Volume Unit, the unit of measurement used by the standard analog VU meter.

3.   What's the best way to avoid lighting the red Over indicators?

The best way to avoid lighting the red Over indicators is to employ a digital brickwall limiter (such as the T-RackS Brickwall Limiter) as the last processor in the signal chain.

4.   Why does the RMS meter always read a lot lower than the Peak meter?

The RMS meter reads the average level of the audio signal, which is about 70 percent of the peak audio signal.

5.   Why do frequencies at 2 to 4 kHz seem louder than the rest of the spectrum?

The human ear is most sensitive to frequencies in the 2- to 4-kHz band, so those frequencies will seem louder when listening to a program where all frequencies are equal in level.

6.   What's the difference between level and loudness?

The difference between level and loudness is the fact that, in mastering, level consists of signal voltages that you read on a meter, while loudness is equivalent to the sound pressure level that you hear.

7.   Why are commercials frequently louder than the television programs around them?

Many television commercials frequently sound louder than the programs that surround them because they're compressed more, so they stand out.

8.   List three examples of where mono might be used.

Typical delivery methods that employ mono audio include AM radio; FM radio when the signal is weak; some television networks; when an MP player, such as iTunes, is configured to play back in mono; or when a stereo song is accidentally ripped in mono.

9.   What can happen if the channels of a song are seriously out of phase?

If the left and right channels of a song are seriously out of phase, any vocals or instruments that are panned to the center may cancel out and disappear from the playback.

10.   How can you tell whether something is out of phase by reading the Phase Scope?

A vertical line reading straight up and down indicates the presence of a mono audio signal when reading the T-RackS Phase Scope.

Chapter 10

1. What is competitive level?

   Trying to make a song sound at least as loud as other commercially released recordings is what's known as competitive level.

2. What is hyper-compression?

   Too much buss compression or compression during mastering leads to hyper-compression, which results in a song being loud but lifeless because the dynamics have been compressed out of it.

3. Why should hyper-compression be avoided at all costs?

   Hyper-compression should be avoided at all costs because it can't be undone, it can make a track sound weak instead of punchy, MP3 encoders may insert unwanted side effects with a hyper-compressed track, it can cause listener fatigue, and it can sound bad over the radio because the hyper-compression will negatively interact with the broadcast processors at the station.

4. What is the normal maximum level setting of the limiter during mastering?

   The normal maximum level setting of the limiter during mastering is −0.1 dB.

5. What is the typical mastering signal chain?

   The typical mastering signal chain consists of an equalizer, a compressor, and a limiter, in that order.

6. Which position in the signal chain will the limiter always be in?

   The limiter must always be placed in the last position of the signal chain in order to prevent digital overs in the audio program.

7. Why is a compressor used in the mastering signal chain?

   The compressor is an essential piece of the mastering signal chain because it raises the relative audio level of the program.

8. What is the look-ahead function of a digital brickwall limiter?

   The look-ahead function delays the audio signal by a small amount (2 milliseconds or so) so that the limiter can anticipate any peaks in the program and catch them before they get by and cause a digital over.

9. What types of sounds are most affected by the Attack Time control on a compressor or limiter?

   Fast transient sounds like that of drums and percussion are most affected by the Attack Time control on a compressor or limiter.

10. What is pumping?

Pumping occurs when the release time is short and not in time with song so the level increases and decreases noticeably.

Chapter 11

1. What is a disadvantage of putting an EQ before a compressor in the signal chain?

The major disadvantage of putting an EQ before a compressor in the signal chain is that if you boost a particular frequency range a great deal (such as 6 dB or more), the compressor will trigger at that frequency rather than the overall frequency envelope of the instrument or vocal. This causes the compressor to sometimes react in an unexpected manner.

2. What's the rule of thumb for EQ/compressor order?

The general rule of thumb for EQ/compressor order is if you're going to use a large amount of EQ, place the EQ after the compressor, and if you're going to use a large amount of compression, place the compressor after the EQ.

3. What is the maximum setting of the Output Ceiling control on the Brickwall Limiter before an overload occurs?

The maximum setting of the Output Ceiling control before overload occurs is −0.1 dB.

4. What controls have the most influence on the sound on the Brickwall Limiter?

The Attack and Release controls have the most influence on the sound on the Brickwall Limiter.

5. What are the general settings of the Attack and Release controls on the Brickwall limiter for a "punchy" sound?

A good starting setting for a "punchy" sound for the Attack control is 5 ms and the Release control at 10 ms. Increase or decrease the Attack control until the audio begins to dull. (It depends upon the type of program.) Increase or decrease the Release control until the audio breathes with the pulse of the track.

6. Why can't you set your compressor and limiter the same for all the songs on an album?

You can't set your compressor and limiter the same for all the songs on an album because each song is unique and has different dynamics, which require different settings.

7. What circumstances call for additional processors besides the main three normally used during mastering?

Rather than push a single processor to the point of distortion or non-linearity, it's better to use multiple processors in order to keep the audio clean, smooth, and punchy.

8. Why would you use M/S mode for mastering?

Using the M/S mode of a processor sometimes allows high-energy signals that are panned to the middle of the stereo spectrum to be separated from the instruments that reside more to the sides of the mix. As a result, M/S mode can sometimes be used to process a single element of the mix rather than the entire mix.

9. Why is the Compare function in T-RackS 3 so important?

It's important to constantly compare your processed audio to the unprocessed audio that you started with to be sure that you're actually improving the song. It's easy to be deceived if one is louder than the other, but the Compare function allows both the processed and unprocessed audio to be instantly compared at the same level so you can really tell the difference.

10. Why would you apply a fade-in at the beginning of a song?

A fade-in is used to smoothly eliminate any noise, count-offs, or coughs before the song begins.

Chapter 12

1. What is an album sequence?

An album sequence is the order of songs as they appear on a CD, online album, or vinyl record.

2. What are spreads?

Spreads are the spacing between songs on an album.

3. What are PQ subcodes?

PQ subcodes are metadata inserted into the digital audio signal on a CD that indicate track timing and location, how many tracks are present, and when to change from track to track, as well as CD-Text, ISRC, and UPC identification codes.

4. Why can't you just export your songs for a CD from your typical DAW if they're placed on a single timeline?

Most DAW timelines don't have the ability to insert the PQ subcodes required to separate the songs on a CD. If 10 songs appeared on the timeline, they would be exported as one long continuous song instead of as 10 individual ones.

5. What is an ISRC code?

    ISRC is short for International Standard Recording Code and is a unique iden-
    tifier for each track. It lists the country of origin, registrant (releasing entity,
    usually the label), year, and designation code (unique identifier created by the
    label).

6. How can you obtain an ISRC code for your songs?

    If you digitally distribute your music through TuneCore or CD Baby, they'll
    automatically assign an ISRC for each song for you. Many CD replicators will
    also assign ISRCs for you, but you can register yourself at usisrc.org so you can
    begin to self-assign ISRC codes to all your music.

7. List three instances where a new ISRC code is required for the same song.

    Whenever a song is changed in any way, it requires a new ISRC code. This means
    a remix, a different mix, or an edited mix of the same song; a rerelease as a
    catalog item; or even multiple takes of the same song from the same recording
    session.

8. What's a UPC code?

    UPC stands for Universal Product Code, which is a number represented by a
    barcode on the back of the packaging of almost any item in any store these days.
    The UPC is used for inventory control and sales tracking.

9. How can you obtain a UPC code for your album?

    You can get a single UPC from CD Baby for $20 if you're already a member or
    from Nationwide Barcode (nationwidebarcode.com) for $10.

10. What is lossy data compression?

    Lossy data compression eliminates certain audio information that the lossy
    encoder believes is unimportant and won't be audibly missed in order to decrease
    the file size.

Index

Course Technology PTR

COURSE CLIPS

Introducing *Course Clips*!

Course Clips are interactive DVD-ROM training products for those who prefer learning on the computer as opposed to learning through a book. *Course Clips Starters* are for beginners and *Course Clips Masters* are for more advanced users.

**Pro Tools 8
Course Clips Master**
Steve Wall ▪ $49.99

**Pro Tools 8
Course Clips Starter**
Steve Wall ▪ $29.99

**Ableton Live 8
Course Clips Master**
Brian Jackson ▪ $49.99

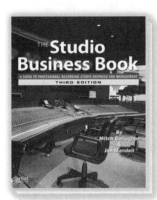
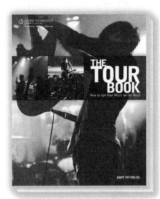
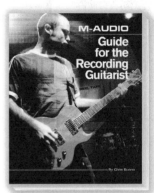